Das Potenzial der kleinen Stadt Litomyšl

The Potential of the Small City of Litomyšl

Edition **DETAIL**

Texte / Essays

Projekte / Projects

„Zuerst die Stadt, dann das Haus" – so das Credo des Architekten Arno Lederer. Damit wird eine Hierarchie von Wertigkeiten benannt, denen dieses Buch folgt. Es fragt freilich auch: Was ist Stadt? Da ist zum einen die konkrete Stadt Litomyšl in Nordböhmen mit ihren 11.000 Einwohnern. Da sind zum anderen Beobachtungen über Art und Maß einer Stadt in Allgemeinen, eingeschlossen die Frage, wann fängt Stadt an, wann hört sie auf. Da ist schließlich die Frage nach der Geschichte und der aktuellen Vitalität dieser Stadt und der Rolle der Architektur. Jedoch: Lederers Feststellung meint mehr: Zwei Dinge sind genannt. Stadt und Haus – beide sind unzertrennlich aufeinander bezogen. Das heißt: Auch um Häuser geht es, alte und neue, und darüber hinaus um den Raum zwischen den Häusern. Damit steht immer auch der Umgang mit Häusern in Rede. Ob Weiterbauen oder Neubauen, ob prominentes Bauwerk oder kleiner Eingriff am Wege – Antworten heutiger Architekten sind gefragt. Litomyšl hat mit seinem Querschnitt zeitgenössischer tschechischer Architektur dazu Außergewöhnliches vorzuweisen. Damit zeigt es, was in solch einem Gemeinwesen steckt; es wird zu einem Muster für das Potential der kleinen Stadt.

"First the town, then the house" – such is the credo of the well-known architect Arno Lederer, and the order of significance on which this book is based. Of course, the question also is: What is a town? On the one hand, there is the specific town of Litomyšl in northern Bohemia, with its 11,000 inhabitants. On the other hand, there are observations about the type and dimensions of a town in general, including the question of: Where does the town begin and where does it end? Finally, there is the issue of the history and current vitality of this town and the role of its architecture. However: Lederer's statement contains more, it mentions two things. Town and house – both are inseparable. This means it is also about houses, old and new; and beyond that, the spaces between the houses. And it is always about the treatment of houses. It doesn't matter whether it is continued or new construction – we are interested in the responses by today's architects. Litomyšl has extraordinary results to show for. This demonstrates what such a community is capable of achieving; it becomes a model for the potential of the small town.

Von Wundern und dergleichen

Of Miracles and Such

Florian Aicher

Außergewöhnliche Ereignisse werden gerne Wunder genannt. Der Architekturtheoretiker Rostislav Švácha hat den Begriff das „Wunder Litomyšl" eingeführt, indem er im Jahr 2001 Litomyšl unter den zahlreichen Städten des Landes mit knapp 10.000 Einwohnern eine eigene Kategorie zusprach. Sein Prager Kollege Zdeněk Lukeš meinte später, wer in der tschechischen Architektur etwas bedeuten will, sollte mindestens ein Projekt in Litomyšl gebaut haben. Einig sind sich Kritiker wie Architekten, dass die tschechische Architektur hier ein neues Zentrum hat.

EINE TSCHECHISCHE STADT

Litomyšl liegt auf 333 m über Meereshöhe am nordöstlichen Rand des böhmischen Kernlandes, nahe der europäischen Wasserscheide und der Sprachgrenze zu Mähren und etwa 50 km südlich des Adlergebirges mit der Grenze zu Polen. Die von fruchtbaren Feldern umgebene Stadt entwickelte sich am östlichen Ufer des kleinen Elbezuflusses Loučná auf zwei ansteigenden Hochebenen.
Auf dem höheren Plateau entstanden im 10. Jahrhundert Burg, Kirche und bald ein Kloster, in dem sich bis in die Neuzeit mehrere Orden abwechselten. Unterhalb entwickelte sich eine Siedlung, die 1259 Stadtrecht erhielt. Eine zweite Kirche wurde gebaut, die Stadt befestigt. Das Gemeinwesen gedieh, bis ab 1421 soziale, politische, sprachliche und religiöse Auseinandersetzungen zu den Hussitenkriegen führten. Der Sieg der Gegenreformation in Litomyšl war verbunden mit dem Namen der Herren von Pernstein. Ab 1567 begann der Bau ihres Renaissanceschlosses durch die Tessiner Architektenfamilie Aostalli. 1640 wurde der Bildungsorden der Piaristen nach Litomyšl berufen, 1714 begann der Bau einer Ordenskirche nach dem Entwurf von Giovanni Battista Alliprandi. Das Wirken des Ordens bescherte dem Ort bedeutende Gelehrte und einen toleranten Geist, der sich ab 1733 in einem philosophischen Institut entfaltete. In diesem Bildungsmilieu gedieh ab 1790 die Idee der nationalen Wiedergeburt Tschechiens, Litomyšl wurde ein Zentrum dieser Bewegung. Wichtige Namen sind mit der Stadt verbunden, so wurde der Komponist Bedřich Smetana hier 1824 geboren. Die Industrialisierung erfasste Litomyšl nicht; die Eisenbahn fuhr ab 1851 wenige Kilometer an der Stadt vorbei. Fortan galt die hier herrschende Leidenschaft der Bildung, Musik und Kunst.
Die Erste Tschechoslowakische Republik ab 1918 änderte daran wenig. Ein neuer Stadtteil mit Wohn-, Verwaltungs- und Schulbauten entstand gegenüber der Altstadt. Trotz der Nähe zu deutschsprachigen Siedlungsgebieten erlebte die vorwiegend von Tschechen bewohnte Stadt ruhige Jahre, die 1938/39 jäh durch die Nazis beendet wurden. Litomyšl beklagte in den folgenden Jahren 150 Widerstandsopfer. Der Befreiung der Tschechen, dem Einmarsch der Roten Armee und ersten freien Wahlen folgte 1948 der Februarumsturz: Die Tschechoslowakei wurde zum wohl eifrigsten stalinistischen Satelliten. Das (Bildungs-)Bürgertum wurde zum Feind, was sich 1950 in Schauprozessen zeigte. Der Hausbesitz der Bürger am Marktplatz wurde verstaatlicht, die Piaristenkirche verfiel, die Synagoge musste Plattenbauten weichen, die verkehrsgerechte Ortsdurchfahrt riss eine große Wunde.

1989

Litomyšl wurde „grau und langweilig". So die Erinnerung des Mannes, der im November 1989 vor 3000 begeisterten Stadtbewohnern auf dem Smetana-Platz den Regimewechsel betrieb. „Auf dem Balkon stand ein einziger Mann, der wusste, wo er hinwollte, der bekam die Leute hinter sich und die Leute haben ihm vertraut. Das war Miroslav Brýdl. Eine moralische Autorität, frei von Korruption", resümiert der Architekt Josef Pleskot. Es waren Tage der Euphorie, die alte Ordnung löste sich auf, regiert wurde informell. Ein Jahr später war Brýdl gewählter Bürgermeister. Er wollte weg vom Grau, hin zu einer vitalen Stadt mit erneuerter Gestalt. Räume und Bauten, Alt und Neu verstand er als Einheit, Architektur als Motor der Stadtentwicklung.
Wie kommt der Ökonom Brýdl, Jahrgang 1941, zu dieser Haltung? Der Prager Frühling und der Einmarsch von Truppen des Warschauer Paktes im August 1968 hatten ihn aufgewühlt, berufliche Einschränkungen waren die Folge. Doch entscheidend war der Impuls aus der Stadt: Seit 1974 wurden die Sgraffiti des Schlosses von vier Prager Künstlern restauriert, die politisch in Ungnade gefallen waren – unter anderem Olbram Zoubek, der Jan Palach nach seiner Selbstverbrennung die Totenmaske abgenommen hatte. Begegnungen waren unvermeidlich. Brýdl war beeindruckt, mit Zoubek stand er

Extraordinary events are often spoken of as miracles. Architectural theorist Rostislav Švácha introduced the term "miracle of Litomyšl" by awarding Litomyšl its own category among the numerous cities of the country with just under 10,000 inhabitants in 2001. His Prague colleague Zdeněk Lukeš later said that anyone who wanted to be of note in Czech architecture should have built at least one project in Litomyšl. Both critics and architects agree that Czech architecture has a new focal point here.

A CZECH TOWN

Litomyšl lies at 333 metres above sea level on the north-eastern edge of the Bohemian heartland, near the European watershed and the language border with Moravia and about 50 km south of the Orlické Mountains on the border with Poland. Surrounded by fertile fields, the town developed on two ascending plateaus on the eastern bank of the small Elbe tributary Loučná.

In the 10th century, a castle, church and soon a monastery, which was successively used by several orders up to the modern era, were built on the higher plateau. Below, a settlement developed that received town rights in 1259. A second church was built and the town was fortified. The community flourished until, from 1421, social, political, linguistic and religious conflicts led to the Hussite Wars. The victory of the Counter-Reformation in Litomyšl can be ascribed to the Lords of Pernstein. The construction of their Renaissance castle by the Aostalli family of architects from Ticino began in 1567. In 1640, the Piarist order of education was called to Litomyšl and, in 1714, the construction of a church for the order according to a design by Giovanni Battista Alliprandi began. The order's work brought distinguished scholars and a spirit of tolerance to the place, which led to the founding of a philosophical institute in 1733. In this intellectual environment, the idea of the Czech National Revival flourished from 1790, and Litomyšl became a centre of this movement. Important names are associated with the town, for example, the composer Bedřich Smetana was born here in 1824. The Industrial Revolution did not affect Litomyšl; from 1851, a railway line passed by a few kilometres from the town. Since then, a passion for education, music and ther arts has prevailed here.

The founding of the First Czechoslovak Republic in 1918 changed little. A new neighbourhood with residential, administrative and school buildings was built opposite the Old Town. Despite its proximity to German-speaking settlement areas, the town's predominantly Czech population experienced quiet years, which were abruptly ended by the Nazis in 1938/39. Litomyšl's resistance suffered 150 casualties over the following years. The liberation of the Czechs, the invasion by the Red Army and the first free elections were followed in 1948 by a coup d'état: Czechoslovakia turned into the arguably most zealous Stalinist satellite. The (intellectual) bourgeoisie became an enemy, as demonstrated by show trials in 1950. The houses owned by citizens on the market square were nationalised, the Piarist church fell into disrepair, the synagogue had to give way to prefabricated housing, and the traffic-friendly through-road tore a large wound in the urban fabric.

1989

Litomyšl became "dull and boring", according to the memories of the man who in November 1989 called for a regime change in front of 3,000 enthusiastic citizens on Smetana Square. "There was just one man on the balcony who knew where he was going. He got people behind him and people trusted him. That was Miroslav Brýdl. A moral authority, free from corruption", says architect Josef Pleskot. This was a time of euphoria, the old order was dissolved, the town informally governed. A year later Brýdl was elected mayor. He wanted to leave the grey behind and create a zestful town with a renewed shape. He considered spaces and buildings, old and new as a whole, and architecture as the engine of urban development.

How did the economist Brýdl, born in 1941, arrive at this position? The Prague Spring and the invasion by Warsaw Pact troops in August 1968 had been deeply unsettling to him, which resulted in occupational restrictions. But a stimulus from the town proved to be decisive: From 1974 on, the sgraffiti of the castle were restored by four Prague artists who had fallen out of favour politically – including Olbram Zoubek, who had taken the death mask of Jan Palach after his self-immolation. Encounters were inevitable. Brýdl was impressed, Zoubek was "on the balcony" with him in

Die Stadt ist ein dichtes Gefüge aus ähnlichen, doch nie gleichen Häusern neben herausragenden Bauten; der Mensch als Fußgänger bleibt ihr Maßstab. Szene am Toulovcovo-Platz (oben).

Episoden der Stadtgeschichte verdichten sich zu vielfältigen, komplexen Erzählungen. Plattenbauten der 1970er-Jahre sind wenige Hundert Meter neben barocker Gartenarchitektur zu sehen (rechts oben).

The town is a dense fabric of often similar but never identical houses next to outstanding buildings; their scale is defined by the human pedestrian. Scene at Toulovcovo Square (above).

Episodes of town history are condensed into diverse, complex narratives. Prefab construction of the 1970s can be found just a few hundred metres from baroque garden architecture (top right).

Die Stadt entwickelt sich als kompakter Körper in enger Begegnung mit dem Land und wird in dieser Gegenüberstellung zur wahrnehmbaren Gestalt. Rechts unten: Litomyšl von Süden.

The town as a compact body develops from its close encounter with the countryside; this juxtaposition gives it a noticeable *gestalt*. Bottom right: Litomyšl from the south.

1989 „auf dem Balkon". 1989 brachte eine Ausstellung viele der späteren Protagonisten in der Stadt zusammen. Freundschaften mit lokalen Künstlern wie Bohdan Kopecký bekamen neue Bedeutung.

ANFANGEN

Bruch und Bestand – beides prägt die Bautätigkeit nach 1989 in Litomyšl. Das lange Vernachlässigte wird zügig und entschieden angegangen. Nach einem Jahr erhält die Stadt eine Stadtarchitektin, Zdeňka Vydrová aus Brünn. Im folgenden Jahr werden bereits drei Wettbewerbe professionell abgewickelt, zwei mit gebauten Resultaten, der dritte wurde zum Auslöser einer wichtigen Debatte. So geht es weiter: Alle anderthalb Jahre wird ein Wettbewerb ausgeschrieben. Im ersten Jahrzehnt entstehen zwei Schulen, die bislang größte Wohnanlage, Sportanlagen, ein zentraler Park, erneuerte Gassen und Plätzen, dazu private Bauten. „Wir wussten: Wenn wir als Stadt gut bauen, bewegen wir auch Privatleute dazu. Wesentlich war: Es muss Niveau haben", so Brýdl. Die Restitution brachte die Eigentümer an den Marktplatz zurück. „Es entstand ein regelrechter Wettbewerb, wer's am besten macht, den schönsten Laden hat. Das haben wir unterstützt und wurden selber gezwungen, mitzuhalten", erinnert sich Jan Janeček, erster Nachfolger Brýdls, und berichtet vom neuen Stolz auf die Stadt. Bauen wurde Gesprächsthema. Es gab Ausstellungen, Ortsbegehungen, Treffen in Wirtshäusern, wo die Projekte mit den Architekten diskutiert wurden. „Der Klostergarten war 2000 der Wendepunkt, der das Vertrauen der Bürger in unsere Arbeit bestätigt hat", erinnert sich Brýdl. Die Resonanz der Medien wirkte bestärkend. Die Euphorie der Wende wirkte lange nach; geplant wurde spontan, direkt. „Heute ist die Bürokratie zurück", so Brýdl.

BEDINGUNGEN

2002 war Miroslav Brýdls Amtszeit zu Ende. Ihm folgte Jan Janeček, vier Jahre später Michal Kortyš, 2014 Radomil Kašpar, 2018 schließlich Daniel Brýdl. Alle Beteiligten heben die Beständigkeit hervor. „Der Wille, das Ganze zu bedenken, umzuwandeln, weiterzuarbeiten mit Aufmerksamkeit für scheinbar kleine Sachen – das macht Litomyšl aus. Man denkt länger als eine Wahlperiode", betont Architekt Aleš Burian.

Beständig war auch die Verwaltung. Der Bauamtsleiter ist seit 25 Jahren tätig, die Stadtarchitektin Zdeňka Vydrová sogar zwei Jahre länger. „Sie vertrat entschieden den Standpunkt des Städtebaus und der Gemeinde gegenüber Investor und Architekt", erinnert sich Michal Kortyš, Bürgermeister von 2006 bis 2014. „Lag dann das Projekt des Architekten vor, hielt sie sich konsequent heraus. Sie war die Polizistin des öffentlichen Raums, ihr ging es darum, dass das Gebäude passt. Sie hat mir enorm den Rücken gestärkt. Ich verlieh ihr umgekehrt institutionelle Macht – Zusammenarbeit auf Basis von Vertrauen."
Bei dem erwähnten Wettbewerb im Jahr 1992 ging es um einen Supermarkt am Marktplatz. Das Siegerprojekt von Pleskot löste eine heftige Debatte über die Balance von Alt und Neu aus, Protest erhob sich. „Mir wurde klar", so Brýdl, „wie schwierig es in der historischen Stadt ist, etwas zu tun. Und die Erkenntnis, neu zu bauen, um zu erhalten, musste reifen". Das Projekt wurde aufgegeben, doch gefestigt war der Wille, in alter Umgebung neu zu bauen. Das gelang zunächst leichter mit Projekten jenseits des klassischen Hochbaus; so die frühe Gestaltung des öffentlichen Raums durch Burian. Verdichtungen sind feststellbar, große Aufmerksamkeit für vermeintliche Nebensächlichkeiten des Alltags. Ein schlichter Eingriff wie die Behebung einer Straßenenge mittels neuer Arkaden durch Pleskot ist „keine große Architektur, nur genial", wie Brýdl sich ausdrückt. Kortyš nennt die Mariánská-Gasse unterhalb des Schlossbergs. Man könnte sie ein Konzentrat der Arbeit Vydrovás nennen, die hier den Stadtraum dem unmittelbaren Zugriff der Verwertung entziehen konnte.
Diese kleinen Eingriffe bilden eine Kontinuität des Raums – unaufgeregte Nutzerfreundlichkeit statt Stil. Die Stadt als Ort wird erlebbar. „Öffentliche Verbindungen suchen, Durchgänge schaffen. Das hat auch vorbereitet, was dann bei Burians Bibliothek oder unserem Museum aufging: Dass man stark in historische Substanz eingreift", so Pleskot. Raum und Zeit greifen ineinander. Radomil Kašpar, zuletzt Bürgermeister, spricht von der Stadt als „Zeitmaschine".

ZEIT DER REIFE

Indem er den Hochwasserschutz zu einem Thema des öffentlichen Raums machte, erschloss Pleskot

1989. Also in 1989, an exhibition brought together many of the later protagonists in the town. Friendships with local artists like Bohdan Kopecký gained new significance.

BEGINNING

Breakage and existing buildings – both shaped the construction activity in Litomyšl after 1989. What had been neglected for a long time was tackled quickly and with determination. A year later, the town had a town architect, Zdeňka Vydrová from Brno. The following year, three competitions were already professionally conducted, two with built results, and the third turned into a catalyst for an important debate. It continued this way: every year and a half, a competition was announced. In the first decade, two schools were built, the largest residential complex to date, sports facilities, a central park, renovated lanes and squares, as well as private buildings. "We knew that if we built well as a town, we would also encourage private individuals to do so. The essential idea was: it has to set a high standard", says Brýdl.

The restitution brought the house owners back to the market square. "A real competition developed between them about who had the best approach and the most beautiful shop. We supported this and were compelled to keep up ourselves", remembers Jan Janeček, Brýdl's direct successor, speaking about the town's newly won pride.

Building became a topic of conversation. Exhibitions, site visits and meetings in pubs were held where the projects were discussed with the architects. "The monastery gardens were the turning point in 2000 that confirmed the citizens' trust in our work", recalls Brýdl. The media response was encouraging. The euphoria of the regime change continued to have an effect for a long time; plans were made spontaneously, directly. "Now bureaucracy is back", says Brýdl.

CONDITIONS

In 2002, Miroslav Brýdl's term ended. He was followed by Jan Janeček, then four years later by Michal Kortyš, in 2014 by Radomil Kašpar, and in 2018 finally by Daniel Brýdl. All involved emphasise the consistency. "The will to think of the whole, to transform, to continue working with attention for seemingly small things – that's Litomyšl. People think beyond their term of office", says architect Aleš Burian.

The administration was also stable. The head of the building department has been active for 25 years, the town architect Zdeňka Vydrová even two years longer. "She would tirelessly argue the viewpoint of town planning and the community towards investors and architects", recalls Michal Kortyš, mayor from 2006 to 2014. "Then, when the architect's project was on the table, she would keep her nose out of it. She was the guardian of public space, her concern was that the building must fit. She supported me enormously. In return, I gave her institutional power – cooperation based on trust."

The 1992 competition mentioned involved a supermarket on the market square. The winning project by Pleskot triggered a heated debate over the balance of old and new, protest was raised. "I realised", says Brýdl, "how difficult it was to do things in the historic town. And it took some time to develop the idea that sustaining the old might have to involve new buildings." The project was abandoned, but the will to rebuild in historic surroundings was now firmly established.

Initially, this was easier with projects beyond classic building construction, for example, the early shaping of the town's public space by Burian. Compression is noticeable in places, as well as great attention for supposed minor matters of everyday life. A simple intervention by Pleskot like widening a narrow bit of a street with new arcades, is "not great architecture, just ingenious", as Brýdl puts it. Kortyš mentions Mariánská Lane below the castle hill. It could be described as the essence of Vydrová's work, who was able to wrest the urban space here from the hands of commercial exploitation.

These small interventions form a continuity of space, down-to-earth user-friendliness rather than style. The town as a place can be experienced. "Search for public connections and create passages. This also prepared what was finally realised at Burian's library or at our museum: that we were able to encroach heavily on the historical substance", says Pleskot. Space and time intertwine. Radomil Kašpar, mayor until recently, speaks of the town as a "time machine".

der Stadt einen vergessenen Grünraum. Ähnliches gilt für den Busknoten südlich der Altstadt. Die Überlassung des Baugrundes an einen Supermarkt war an anspruchsvolle Architektur, ein neues Buswartehaus und einen Park geknüpft. Public Private Partnership (PPP) nach Litomyšler Art. Von öffentlicher Bedeutung ist auch das neue Hallenbad oder Litomyšls einziger Kirchenneubau.

Mit dem EU-Beitritt 2004 war umfangreiche Förderung zu erwarten. Der Schlossberg mit Renaissanceschloss (seit 1999 Unesco-Welterbe) und das Piaristenkloster wurden Thema. Innerhalb von vier Jahren wurden Teile des Schlosses und der Schlossbrauerei, das Piaristenkolleg und seine Kirche sowie das Museum saniert, umgebaut, erweiterter Nutzung angepasst sowie umgebende Plätze neu gestaltet. Dass das Schloss noch immer unvollendet ist, obwohl ein Wettbewerb mit baureifem Projekt vorlag, lässt die Probleme bei der Abwicklung erahnen.

Die Renovierungen auf dem Schlossberg machen wie unterm Brennglas sichtbar, was für die Stadt im Ganzen gilt. Architektur schafft Vielfalt – ein Wert für sich. Pleskot betont: „Schöpferisch umwandeln, Substanz verwenden – Direktheit des Zugriffs." Burian ergänzt: „Wenn wir die Substanz mit Respekt und Sorgfalt geprüft haben und nicht sichtbar eingreifen, sind wir nicht Partner auf Augenhöhe." Noch radikaler sind Petr Hájek, Tomáš Hradečný und Jan Šépka von HŠH architekti: Der purifizierten Substanz stellen sie unvermittelt Einbauten als Antithese entgegen.

BEZIEHUNGEN

Der Bezug auf die Avantgarde der ersten Hälfte des 20. Jahrhunderts vereint die hier wirkenden Architekten. Für Rotislav Švácha gründet darin eine Strenge, die die Architektur des Landes nach 1989 von der seiner Nachbarn unterscheidet. Seinen Ausführungen pflichtet der Architekturhistoriker Pavel Halík bei: „Es scheint, dass die Architektur bei uns weiterhin als eine traditionelle kulturelle Disziplin angesehen wird und dass die tschechische Strenge mehr auf der Vertiefung dieser kulturellen Natur des architektonischen Schaffens gründet als auf einer begeisterten Aufnahme noch nicht verdauter Formen." Zu differenzieren gilt zwischen den beiden Architekturpolen Prag und Brünn. Während hier der Bezug zum Wien Otto Wagners und Adolf Loos' spürbar ist, zeigen sich dort vitalistische Tendenzen mit Vorliebe für Paris. „Brünn ist positivistisch, gebildet. Prag sucht Tiefgang zwischen Seele und Ratio", so Burian. Tatsächlich findet man heute diese beiden Pole in starken Persönlichkeiten ausgeglichen vertreten.

AUSBLICK

Wenn der heutige Bürgermeister Daniel Brýdl feststellt: „Litomyšl ist eine europäische Stadt für Tschechien", dann mit der Einschränkung: „Wir freuen uns über all' die Gäste, aber wir wollen kein Museum werden, sondern eine Stadt bleiben für die Leute, die hier wohnen." Auch er, der nun die Nach-89er-Generation vertritt, sagt: „Das Bauen ist Gewinn für die Stadt: Architektur repräsentiert Werte, kultiviert die Gemeinde und die Beziehung der Bürger. Die Jungen interessieren sich, ziehen nicht weg. Litomyšl ist die einzige Stadt weit und breit, die einen jährlichen Zuwachs hat – in den letzten Jahren rund 270 Personen. Größe und Proportion des Gemeinwesens stimmen. Alles ist da, politische Teilnahme ist jedem möglich, die Wege sind – auch im übertragenen Sinn – kurz. Das schafft Identifikation mit der Stadt, positiven Patriotismus. Die gebildete Mittelschicht, Ingenieure, Wissenschaftler, Mediziner, wächst; die bauen hier."

Also baut er wie seine Vorgänger – etwa eine größere Behindertenwohnanlage. Der Verkehr ist auch hier ein Problem. Der Hauptplatz soll durch einen zentrumsnahen Parkplatz entlastet werden, der Durchgangsverkehr durch eine neue Fußgängerüberführung gemildert. Thema Wohnen: Einige Baugebiete in verdichteter Bauweise mit begrüntem öffentlichen Raum werden entwickelt, doch beim Bauland verfügt die Gemeinde über wenige Reserven. „Das hat einen Vorteil", so Brýdl: „Die Stadt wird dichter, die Lücken werden genutzt, Umbau erwogen. Im Zentrum werden zwei Wohnbauten entstehen, dazu Umbauten einstiger Gewerbebauten." Auch wird das Zentrum durch Renovierung neue kulturelle Einrichtungen erhalten. Heute gibt es Krankenhäuser, Labore, Sportstätten, acht Schulen, sechs Veranstaltungshallen, zwei Museen, sieben Galerien, sieben Festivals, darunter die renommierten Smetana-Festspiele.

Wie sagt Daniel Brýdl, heute Bürgermeister? „Uns fehlt nichts in dieser Stadt."

AGE OF MATURITY

By turning flood protection into an issue of public space, Pleskot opened up a forgotten green space for the town. The same applies to the bus station south of the Old Town. The surrender of the site to a supermarket was linked to the condition of sophisticated architecture, a new waiting hall and a park. Public Private Partnership (PPP) in the Litomyšl way. Also of public importance are the new indoor swimming pool and Litomyšl's only new church building.

With the accession to the EU in 2004, extensive funding was to be expected. The castle hill with its Renaissance castle (UNESCO World Heritage since 1999) and the Piarist monastery were tabled. Within four years, parts of the castle and the castle brewery, the Piarist college and its church and the museum were renovated, altered, adapted to extended use and the surrounding squares were redesigned. The fact that the castle is still unfinished even though there was a building-ready project resulting from a competition hints at the problems in implementation.

The renovations on the castle hill put into focus what applies to the town as a whole. Architecture creates diversity – a value in itself. Pleskot emphasises: "Transform creatively, use existing substance – make direct interventions." Burian adds: "If we have examined the substance with respect and care and do not intervene visibly, we are not partners at eye level." Petr Hájek, Tomáš Hradečný and Jan Šépka from HŠH architekti are even more radical. They abruptly confront the purified substance with antithetical fixtures.

RELATIONSHIPS

Admiration for the avant-garde of the first half of the 20th century unites the architects working here. For Rotislav Švácha, this explains a rigour that distinguishes the architecture of the country after 1989 from that of its neighbours. Architectural historian Pavel Halík agrees with his remarks: "It appears that architecture continues to be seen as a traditional cultural discipline here and that Czech rigour is based more on deepening this cultural nature of architectural creation than on enthusiastically taking in forms that have not yet been digested." However, it is necessary to distinguish between the two architectural poles of Prague and Brno. With one, the relation to the Vienna of Otto Wagner and Adolf Loos is noticeable, while the other shows vitalist tendencies with a preference for Paris. "Brno is positivist and educated. Prague seeks depth between soul and ratio", says Burian.

In strong personalities, both poles are well represented today.

OUTLOOK

Current mayor Daniel Brýdl declares: "Litomyšl is a European town for the Czech Republic". However, he adds: "We welcome all the guests, but we do not want to turn into a museum, we want to remain a town for the people who live here." As a representative of the post-89 generation, he also says: "Building is a gain for the town: Architecture represents values, cultivates the community and the relationships between citizens. The young people are interested, they do not move away. Litomyšl is the only town far and wide that is growing continuously – in recent years by around 270 citizens. The size and proportion of the community are right. Everything is there and political participation is possible for everyone, while distances are short, also in the figurative sense. This creates identification with the town, positive patriotism. The educated middle class of engineers, scientists, and physicians is growing; they are building here."

So, he builds like his predecessors – for example, a larger housing complex for the disabled. Traffic is also a problem here. The main square is to be relieved by a parking lot close to the town centre, transit traffic to be alleviated by a new pedestrian overpass and, in future, a bypass road. The topic of housing: Some densely designed areas with green public spaces are being developed, but the municipality has very few reserves of building land. "This has an advantage", says Brýdl. "The town is becoming more dense, gaps are used, and reconstruction is considered. In the centre, two residential buildings will be built and former commercial buildings altered." Through renovation, the centre will also receive new cultural facilities.

Today, there are hospitals, laboratories, sports facilities, eight schools, six event halls, two museums, seven galleries and seven festivals.

As the current mayor Daniel Brýdl puts it: "We are not lacking anything in this town."

Die neue tschechische Architektur entfaltet sich vor einem reichen Hintergrund. Historische Monumente und Alltagsbauten bezeugen ihr kulturelles und geschichtliches Umfeld. Die spätmittelalterliche Bürgerstadt erlebte den Einbruch der Moderne mit den Bauten der Gründerzeit: Der 1919 begründete Staat suchte dann im Rondokubismus einen eigenen Stil.

The new Czech architecture unfolds against a rich background; historical monuments and everyday buildings attest to their cultural and historical environment. The late medieval town experienced the onset of modernity with the buildings of the *Gründerzeit* era; the state founded in 1919 then sought its own style in rondocubism.

Ab Mitte der 1920er-Jahre knüpft der Funktionalismus nicht zuletzt an die Ökonomiebauten des Schlosses und deren zeitlose Architektur stilistischer Reduktion zwischen 1750 und 1850 an.

From the mid-1920s onwards, functionalism drew on the example of the castle's economic structures and their timeless, stylistically pared-down architecture from between 1750 and 1850.

Das Technische Kolleg nach dem Entwurf von Karel Tymich (ab 1924).

The Technical College designed by Karel Tymich (from 1924).

Die Architekturerneuerer ab 1989 knüpfen oft an die reduzierte Architektursprache des Funktionalismus an. Dies gilt auch für die Masaryk-Schule der Architekten Burian-Křivinka (ab 1994).

The architecture innovators after 1989 often refer to the pared-down architectural language of functionalism. This is also true for the Masaryk School by Burian-Křivinka architects (from 1994).

Stadt im Aufbruch

Florian Aicher im Gespräch mit Tomáš Valena

Town on the Move

Florian Aicher in Conversation with Tomáš Valena

In ausgedehnten Streifzügen näherten sich Tomáš Valena (TV) und Florian Aicher (FA) im Sommer 2018 dem Phänomen Litomyšl an. Als Architekturhistoriker und -theoretiker widmete Tomáš Valena dem Verhältnis von Typus und Topos sowie der Beziehung zwischen Stadt und Landschaft grundlegende Publikationen sowie die Schwerpunkte seiner Lehre an der Hochschule für angewandte Wissenschaften in München. Im Februar 2019 ist der gebürtige Tscheche und Experte des Werks von Josef Plečnik verstorben.

FA Architekten sagen gern: der Raum. Dagegen gibt Heidegger zu bedenken: „Es gibt nicht die Menschen und außerdem den Raum ... der Mensch lebt, indem er sich im Verhältnis zu den Menschen und den Dingen aufhält". Lakonischer drückt das Aldo van Eyck aus: „Was immer Raum und Zeit bedeuten, Ort und Gelegenheit bedeuten mehr."

TV Orte, Dinge – das sind bei Heidegger fast Synonyme. Was wir anfassen, anschauen, riechen, hören, umwandeln – das bedingt uns. Ich halte mich an Leon Battista Alberti, der den Begriff „regio" so bestimmt: Was man vom Bauplatz übersieht, so weit das Auge reicht. Das kann Ortschaft, Siedlung, Stadt sein. Dieses Gefüge von Orten macht das Spezifische der Stadt aus.

FA So weit das Auge reicht ... Ort hat also eine Mitte und eine Grenze.

TV Etwa Plätze mit ihrer Randbebauung. Die Mitte kann frei bleiben oder durch einen Körper gebildet werden, oft ist beides kombiniert. Der Smetana-Brunnen und der Rathausturm auf dem Stadtplatz von Litomyšl bilden eine Balance, ausgewogen und entspannt. Die genannten Eigenschaften sind Gestaltqualitäten. Ort – Christian Norberg-Schulz insistiert darauf – ist existenznotwendig, da er uns Orientierung gibt. Damit bin ich beim Weg, beides hängt eng zusammen. Ort und Weg, das ist Welterfahrung, Fuß-Fassen in der Welt. Zu unterscheiden wären: Raum-Ort und Körper-Ort. Im ersten Fall bin ich Teil des Ortes, von ihm umfangen; im zweiten tritt er mir gegenüber.

FA ... situative Orte, die sich zum Gefüge der Stadt Litomyšl entfalten. Das geht über das unmittelbar Anschauliche hinaus – Bezüge stellen sich her, Erlebtes macht sich geltend.

TV Damit erweitern wir den Begriff dahingehend, was Kevin Lynch mit Erinnerbarkeit zu fassen suchte. Ein städtischer Bereich, ein Viertel konstituiert sich in der Erinnerung der Bewohner als Ort– in Litomyšl die Oberstadt, die Bürgerstadt, die Vorstadt. Dimension wird da wichtig. Wie weit reicht meine Konzentration? Wird der Bereich zu groß, zu heterogen, so ermüdet der Nutzer – auch, wenn er zu monoton wird. Der Schluss liegt nahe, einen zeitlichen Bewegungskreis zu ziehen; etwa, was sich in 10 bis 15 Minuten zu Fuß bewältigen lässt. Wir sind – da folge ich Rudolf Schwarz – in erster Linie Fußgänger. Mühelos bewältigen wir unter normalen Umständen etwa 1000 Meter. Dann ermüden wir, die Konzentration lässt nach. Bei nicht-großstädtischer Bebauungsdichte leben in so einem Umkreis 15.000 bis 30.000 Bewohner.

FA Das ist eine kleine Stadt.

TV Das sind Näherungswerte. Wichtig ist Aufmerksamkeit. Man will unterhalten werden, sucht abwechslungsreiche Erdgeschosszonen, belebten Nahbereich. Ort wird Ortschaft, Bild und Topografie: Weiter oben liegt der Bereich klerikaler und profaner Macht mit Piaristenkirche, Kolleg und Schloss mit Wirtschaftsbauten. Zum anschließenden Klostergarten bemerken wir eine erste Höhenstufe, der Blick weitet sich, die Dächer der bürgerlichen Unterstadt kommen in den Blick. Darüber, in der Ferne, Landwirtschaftsflächen. Je feiner die Topografie ist, umso mehr gilt: Gelände wird man im Gehen gewahr, spürt Brüche und Schwellen, die wechselnden Niveaus wechselnder Bedeutung.

FA Einsichten nach Art des Promenadologen Lucius Burckhardt. Ganz spezifisch und doch typisch.

TV Typisch die Entfaltung von Lage und Ort, lokal, historisch ihre Entfaltung. Oben der räumlich konzentrierte Ort der Macht. Unterhalb der Hangkante erste Formen der Handwerkerstadt. Dann die Terrasse über dem Tal, auf der sich die Bürgerstadt herausbildet mit dem charakteristischen, den Höhenlinien folgenden Platz: lang

In the summer of 2018, Tomáš Valena (TV) and Florian Aicher (FA) approached the Litomyšl phenomenon in extensive walks. As an architectural historian and theorist, Tomáš Valena had dedicated fundamental publications to the relationship between type and topos as well as to the relationship between town and landscape, which also formed the focus of his teaching at the University of Applied Sciences in Munich. The native Czech and expert on Josef Plečnik's work died in February 2019.

FA Architects tend to speak of: space. Heidegger, on the other hand, pointed out that "there isn't man and space in addition ... man lives by being in relation to people and things". Aldo van Eyck put it more laconically: "Whatever space and time mean, place and opportunity mean more."

TV Places, things – to Heidegger, they were almost synonymous. What we touch, look at, smell, hear, transform – that is what determines us. I agree with Leon Battista Alberti, who defined the term "regio" as follows: what you can observe from the building site as far as the eye can see. This can be a village, a settlement, a town. The fabric of places makes up the specific of the town.

FA As far as the eye can see ... So, place has a centre and a limit.

TV For example, squares with their surrounding buildings. The centre can remain free or be formed by a body, often both are combined. The Smetana Fountain and the town hall's tower on Litomyšl's central square create an equilibrium, well-balanced and restful. The properties mentioned are design qualities. Place – as Christian Norberg-Schulz insists – is necessary for existence because it gives us orientation. This brings me to pathways, since both are closely related. Place and pathway are the basis for world experience, for gaining a foothold in the world. We must distinguish between space-place and body-place. In the first case, I am part of the place, surrounded by it; in the second, it is facing me.

FA ... situational places that develop into the fabric of the town of Litomyšl. This goes beyond what is immediately visible – connections become apparent, experiences are asserted.

TV This adds to the concept of what Kevin Lynch termed memorability. An urban area, a neighbourhood, is constituted as a place in the memory of its inhabitants – in Litomyšl those are the upper town, the civil town, the suburbs. Dimension becomes important there. How far will I be able to keep my focus up? If an area becomes too large and too heterogeneous, its users grows tired – also if it becomes too monotonous. This suggests marking out a radius that we are capable of crossing within a certain period; for example, an area that can be negotiated by foot in 10 to 15 minutes. We are – I agree with Rudolf Schwarz here – primarily pedestrians. Under normal circumstances, we cope with distances of about 1,000 metres quite effortlessly. Then we tire and lose focus. In a non-metropolitan building density, 15,000 to 30,000 inhabitants live within such a radius.

FA That is a small town.

TV These are approximate values. Attention is the important factor. You want to be entertained, you seek varied ground floor areas, lively surroundings. Place becomes a locality, image and topography: higher up is the area of clerical and secular power with the Piarist church, the college and the castle with its farm buildings. Towards the adjoining monastery gardens, we notice a first step in height, the view widens, the roofs of the civic lower town come into view. Above, in the distance, agricultural land.
The finer the topography is, the more it is true that terrain becomes noticeable when you walk. You feel breaks and thresholds, the alternating levels of changing significance.

FA Insights according to the promenadologist Lucius Burckhardt. Highly specific and yet typical.

TV The development of location and place is typical, it is local, historical. Above, a spatially concentrated place of power. Below the slope,

Charakteristisch für Litomyšl ist die Polarität von Schlossberg und tiefer liegender Bürgerstadt. Unterhalb der Hangkante siedelten sich Handwerker und Händler an. Die Stadt dehnt sich ab dem Frühbarock aus und erhält mit dem Stadtplatz ein eigenes Zentrum.

What is distinctive of Litomyšl is the polarity of the castle hill and the lower-lying civil town. Below the slope, craftsmen and traders settled. The town began to expand from the early baroque period and, with the town square, was given its own centre.

Diese Stadtstruktur ist vom Salzach-Inn-Raum bis Nordböhmen anzutreffen. Sie bildet einen Typus, der durch den jeweiligen Topos variiert wird. Die Stadtplätze haben geschlossene Wände, vielfach verbunden durch Laubengänge mit Arkaden.

Eine Seitengasse des Stadtplatzes erregt besonderes Aufsehen: Haushohe Sgraffiti – Übertragung von Buchillustrationen von Josef Vachal – bezeugen die Wertschätzung dieses Malerdissidenten seit der Samtenen Revolution (Seite 26).

This town structure can be found from the Salzach-Inn area to northern Bohemia; it forms a type that is varied by the respective topos. The town squares have closed walls, often connected by arcades. A lane leading away from the town square contains a special sensation: full-height sgraffiti – a transfer of book illustrations by Josef Vachal – testify to the esteem in which this dissident painter was held since the Velvet Revolution (page 26).

ROSA
Zahrádkařské potřeby

gezogen, ein Doppelplatz, der sich mittig zusammenzieht und mit dem Rathausturm in die Höhe strebt, an den Enden sich weitet, geometrisch komplex in fast regelmäßigen Kreissegmenten. Gefasst ist der Platz durch zweigeschossige, giebelständige Steinhäuser mit oft waagrechten Blendgiebeln als Abschluss der Grabendächer, die Fassaden mit meist drei Fenster- und zwei Arkadenachsen – eine Bebauung, die sich seit der Renaissance herausbildete.

FA Typologie und Topologie – zwei Wirkkräfte städtischer Entwicklung.

TV Wobei es darauf ankommt, wie Typus auf Topos reagiert. Stadtstruktur entwickelt sich im Wechselspiel und entfaltet so individuelle, konkrete Eigenarten.

FA Das Allgemein-Typische und das Besondere, Herausragende. Die Städtebauliteratur spricht vom Figur-Grund-Phänomen. Dabei ist der Grund keineswegs zweitrangig. Colin Rowe spricht von dem Kippbild Figur-Grund, seiner Wechselwirkung. Städtebaulich steht anonyme Architektur den Monumenten der Hochkultur nicht nach. Anschaulich sind Grund wie Figur.

TV Das Monument, die Figur, braucht den hinreichend großen Grund aus Parzellen, Bauten, Details. Damit Gebautes Ort wird, ist Gleichförmigkeit in Maßen nötig. Das ist positiv und formbildend. Doch es gilt zu differenzieren: Die industrielle Serie erzeugt identische Elemente, handwerkliche Wiederholung dagegen Variation. Das zeigt der Stadtplatz von Litomyšl, soweit der materielle Genius Loci von Litomyšl. Gibt es einen geistigen? Es fällt auf, wie präsent Bildung hier ist – mit vielen Schulen, einer Universitätsfakultät, Verlagen und Persönlichkeiten aus Wissenschaft, Literatur und Kunst. Dass Bedřich Smetana aus Litomyšl kommt, die Wiedergeburt Tschechiens starke Resonanz fand, dass sich Künstler wie Olbram Zoubek hier niederließen – ist das Zufall? Es gibt eine Belebung bis in die bürgerliche Mitte hinein, auch das ist der Genius Loci dieser Stadt.

FA Profitieren die Vorstädte davon?

TV Immer weniger. Jedes Wohnhaus will einzigartig sein, gerade die Parzellen gleichen sich noch. Wo bleibt Gemeinsamkeit? Was sind noch herausragende Bauten? Schulen? Supermärkte? Dazwischen finden wir Wohnbebauung, strukturiert, um Höfe mit Kinderspielplatz konzentrierte Figuren, die sich typologisch und funktionell abheben. Doch das erfordert entschiedenen Zugriff der Kommune oder eines weitsichtigen Bauträgers und dringend Erfahrung in Architektur. Litomyšl wird ein Zentrum neuer tschechischer Architektur genannt – für Einzelbauten gilt das unbestritten. Doch Städtebau mit Gestaltqualität findet man bestenfalls in Ansätzen. Etwas anderes fällt auf, man könnte sagen: Akupunktur. Der Bürgermeister weiß: Der gezielte Zugriff im kleinen Maßstab kann Wirkung entfalten. Wir finden hier vorbildlichen Umgang mit der Bausubstanz und viel mehr. Der Genius Loci bekäme so eine erweiterte, geistige Bedeutung – als kulturelle Ausstrahlung dieser kleinen Stadt.

FA Auffallend sind Eingriffe, die sich mit vermeintlich Nebensächlichem befassen – das Ufer der Loučná, Passagen, Wege, Brunnen, Geländer. Das wirkt im Organismus dieser Stadt.

TV Die Stadt als Ganzes ist Figur, die dem Umland Identität verleiht. Man ist sich der Geschichte bewusst. Mit begrenzten Mitteln und richtigen Ideen wurden das Bauen und der öffentliche Raum erneuert und so neue Nutzungen und Menschen in die Stadt gezogen.

FA Beispiel Regionalmuseum: Das alte Piaristenkolleg wurde nicht nur gekonnt renoviert, sondern mit dem Umgriff, dem neuen Eingang, dem vorgelegten Platz derart in Szene gesetzt, wie es nie zuvor war.

TV Aus dieser kontextuellen Auseinandersetzung entsteht neue Qualität, also viel mehr als brave Erhaltung. Potenzial wird aufgedeckt und entfaltet, Bestand wird verwandelt, alt wird neu.

FA Mit Bruno Latour ausgedrückt: „Nicht Erneuerung, sondern Vergegenwärtigung tut not."

TV Miroslav Šik würde sagen: Alt wird neu, indem es durch Fremdes neu interpretiert, zu Leben

early forms of the craftsmen's town. Then the terrace above the valley, on which the civil town emerges with the characteristic square following the contour lines: an elongated double square that contracts in the middle and ascends with the town hall's tower, while widening at the ends, geometrically complex in almost regular circle segments. The square is surrounded by two-storey, gabled stone houses with often horizontal blind gables as conclusion of the multi-gable roofs, the facades with mostly three windows and two arcade axes – a development that has formed since the Renaissance.

FA Typology and topology – two forces of urban development.

TV Though it depends on how type reacts to topos. Urban structure evolves from interplay and thus develops individual, concrete peculiarities.

FA The general, typical and the special, outstanding. The urban design literature speaks of the figure-ground phenomenon. And the ground is by no means secondary here. Colin Rowe speaks of the tilting figure-ground, its interaction. In terms of urban planning, anonymous architecture is not inferior to the monuments of high culture. Both ground and figure are illustrative.

TV The monument or figure requires a reasonably large ground of plots, buildings, details. In order for buildings to become a place, uniformity in moderation is necessary. That is positive and formative. But it is necessary to distinguish here: the industrial series produces identical elements, while repetition of craftsmanship produces variation. This is demonstrated by the town square of Litomyšl, the material genius loci of Litomyšl. Is there a spiritual one too? It is striking how strongly present education is here – with many schools, a university faculty, publishers and personalities from science, literature and art. The fact that Bedřich Smetana comes from Litomyšl, that the Czech National Revival was very well received, that artists like Olbram Zoubek settled here – is that a coincidence? We have a revival that extends into the civic middle class. That is also the genius loci of this town.

FA Do the suburbs benefit from this?

TV Less and less so. Every house wants to be unique, but the plots are still the same. Where is the common ground? Which buildings can still be called outstanding? Schools? Supermarkets? In between, we find residential buildings, structured, concentrated figures around courtyards with a children's playground that stand out typologically and functionally. But this requires firm guidance from the municipality or a farsighted developer and, very importantly, experience in architecture. Litomyšl is called a hotspot of new Czech architecture – for individual buildings this is unquestionably so. But urban design with *gestalt* quality can be found at best in rudimentary form. There is something else, however, that is striking – let's call it acupuncture. The mayor knows: targeted interventions on a small scale can have an impact. Here we find an exemplary approach towards the building fabric and much more. The genius loci would thus have an expanded, spiritual meaning – as cultural appeal of this small town.

FA There are striking interventions that deal with supposedly trifling matters – the banks of the Loučná, passages, paths, fountains, banisters. This has an impact on the town's organism.

TV The town as a whole is a figure that gives the surrounding areas identity. One is aware of its history. With limited resources and the right kind of ideas, buildings and public space were renewed, bringing new uses and people to the town.

FA For example, the Regional Museum: The old Piarist college was not only skilfully renovated but, with the placing of its new entrance and the square in front, was presented as never before.

TV New quality arises from this contextual approach, which is so much more than faithful preservation. Potential is revealed and developed, existing stock is transformed, old becomes new.

FA In Bruno Latour's words: "Not renewal but a bringing to mind is what is needed."

Die Wege der Stadt sind nicht auf funktionale Zwecke reduziert. Alte Verbindungen wurden durch neue ergänzt und erweitert. Sie fügen sich in das Netz alter Gassen und sind auch für unterschiedliche Verkehrsteilnehmer gedacht.

The town's pathways are not reduced to functional purposes. Old connections were supplemented and extended by new ones that fit in seamlessly with the network of old streets and are sometimes intended for different types of users.

Die Variationen reichen von Platzwegen bis zu Wasserspielplätzen oder sonstigen kleinen Eingriffen, die das Netz alter Gassen erweitern, Übergänge eröffnen und Beziehungen schaffen.

The variations range from paths across squares to water playgrounds or other small interventions that extend the network of old streets, open transitions and create relationships.

erweckt wird. Und das geschieht hier mit genauem Gespür für den Ortsbezug. Der spitze, flache Eingangsbau von Pleskot gibt Blickbezüge frei, verdankt seine Form auch dem Umfeld. Die Erweiterung des Piaristenkollegs durch Burian belebt durch Kontrast in Material und Geometrie. Zwei Architektenstatements in Spannung zueinander. Besonders fasziniert mich der Bereich der Hangkante, der Übergang von der Ober- zur Unterstadt. Mir scheint, da legt Burian wie eine Spinne seine Fäden aus, verknüpft hier eine Enge, da ein Plätzchen. Vieles bleibt offen, Unspektakuläres kommt in den Blick, Gelassenheit entsteht. Der Natur verbleiben Spielräume.

FA Damit sind wir am Wasser: Auf gesamter Länge begleitet die Loučná die Kernstadt. Ein kleiner Fluss im schattigen Grün seiner Auen wurde wach geküsst.

TV Was vor 18 Jahren als Hochwasserschutz begann, verwandelt Pleskot in eine Besitzergreifung des Stadtflusses durch seine Bürger, indem er Eingriffe im Sinne Plečniks vornimmt: eine „Platzbrücke", Treppenanlagen vom schmalen Stieg bis hin zu ausgedehnten Sitzstufen, „Wildwechsel" im Gehölz, eine Terrassenbastion. Pleskot war seinerzeit mit dem Jelení příkop, dem Hirschgraben, auf der Prager Burg befasst. Damit wird Bezug gesucht zu dem Gestalter des 20. Jahrhunderts, der wie kein anderer mit öffentlichem Raum Stadt gebaut hat – mit starken Gesten und kaum Wahrnehmbarem. Der Bürgermeister bestätigt, wie inspirierend seinerzeit Plečniks Interventionen für ihn waren. Doch Zeit und Umstände sind andere. Pleskots Platzbrücke wirkt mitunter verloren, manches wirkt schematisch; stark dagegen seine lakonische, rohe Sprache, fast brüsk ...

FA Ein Jahrzehnt später setzen Rusina Frei Architekti die Ufergestaltung fort, die Handschrift wirkt lockerer. Das Smetana-Haus am anderen Ufer strahlt aus, ein gut besuchter Spielplatz garantiert Publikum.

TV Das Zusammenspiel beider Ufer klappt dank offenen Geländes und lichten Grüns. Die Spielgeräte sind künstlerische Unikate – wo gibt es sonst so hohe Qualität?

Doch mich zieht es zurück zur Geländekante in der Stadt. Da finde ich das Spezifische, den Ortsbezug, die architektonische Qualität, die Bewältigung der Topografie. Beginnend mit der Passage am Ortseingang, die lapidar die Qualität der Lauben aufgreift. Dann der schwebende Gehweg in weitem Radius hinauf, ein Schwung der einige Gassen weiter mit der Treppeanlage um die zweite Kirche sein Echo findet.

FA Und der Brunnen am Fuß der Hangkante: sinnfälliger Ort einer Quelle, gefasst durch barockes Gewände. Das Wasser ergießt sich aufs Trottoir, wird durch wenige Steinschnitte umgelenkt in ein Becken, gefasst durch Steinbank und Steg mit Handlauf. Wie das den alten Waschplatz vergegenwärtigt: Wir sahen eine Anwohnerin ihren Türvorleger waschen. Keine Behübschung, sondern Gebräuchlichkeiten ernst nehmen – so stimmt's.

TV Diese Bearbeitung der Gassen und Plätze durch Burian erfolgt durch individuelle Eingriffe. Mit der Neugestaltung des Außenraums um das Schloss und die Piaristenkirche durch Pleskot ergibt das ein Ganzes – gefügt aus Beiträgen wechselnder Autoren in vielen Schritten, umgesetzt im Lauf von 20 Jahren.

FA Dank Akupunktur unterhalb einer „großen" Planung. Das bleibt spannend, öffnet Potenziale, ohne abzuschließen, belässt Fragmente, erlaubt Entwicklung ...

TV ... voraussetzt, es hat Kraft. Das hat Plečnik gezeigt – nicht zuletzt mit der Üppigkeit seiner Formen. Die stehen den heutigen Architekten kaum mehr zur Verfügung. Da geht's bescheidener zu Werk, auch direkter – etwa mit dem Bottich vor Pleskots Museumseingang. Plecnik wollte den Fußgänger unterhalten, Reize, Bilder, Geschichten bieten. So auch Pleskot – das ist nicht abstrakt, da werde ich angesprochen.

FA Da darf der große Brunnen im neuen Klostergarten von Babka/Květ/Sendler mit den Figuren von Zoubek nicht fehlen. An heißen Tagen zeigt sich, wie unmittelbar Kinder aufgreifen, was ganz anschaulich vorliegt. Ist diese Unmittelbarkeit ein Schlüssel für diesen Kulturkreis?

TV Miroslav Šik would say: Old becomes new by being reinterpreted and brought to life by the other. And that is combined here with a good feeling for the place and its references. The pointed, flat entrance building by Pleskot opens up visual axes, owing its form also to its surroundings. The extension of the Piarist college by Burian animates through contrast in material and geometry. Two architect's statements in tension with each other. I am particularly fascinated by the slope area, the transition from upper to lower town. It is as if Burian were spinning his threads like a spider, linking a narrow passage here with a little square there. Much remains open, unspectacular parts come into view, serenity is the result. Nature is left with scope for movement.

FA Which brings us to the water: the Loučná flows along the entire length of the core town. A small river in the shady green of its meadows was kissed awake.

TV What began as flood protection 18 years ago, has been transformed by Pleskot into an appropriation of the town's river by its citizens, thanks to interventions in the sense of Plečnik: a "square on a bridge", stairs ranging from a narrow staircase to extended seating steps, "game paths" in the woods, a terrace on a bastion. Pleskot was at that time concerned with the Jelení příkop, the deer moat, at the Prague Castle. In this way, reference is made to the designer of the 20th century who used public space to develop cities like no one else – with strong gestures and barely noticeable ones. The mayor has confirmed how inspiring Plečnik's interventions were to him at the time. But our time and its circumstances are different now. Pleskot's square on a bridge sometimes appears almost lost, some parts feel schematic; his laconic, raw, almost brusque language, on the other hand, is powerful ...

FA A decade later, Rusina Frei Architekti continue the design of the banks, and their signature has a looser feel. The Smetana House on the other bank has a radiating effect, a well-attended playground guarantees an audience.

TV The interaction of the two banks works thanks to an open terrain and sparse greenery. The play equipment is unique – where else is there such high quality?
But I am drawn back to the edge of the terrain in the town. There I find the specific, the location, the architectural quality, the coping with the topography. Starting with the passage at the town's entrance, which succinctly takes up the quality of the arbours. Then the pavement wafting upwards in a wide radius and, in the sweep of the stairs around the second church, finding its echo in some lanes.

FA And the fountain at the foot of the slope: a place suggestive of a spring, surrounded by baroque embrasure. The water pours onto the pavement, is diverted by a few stone cuts into a pool, framed by a stone bench and a footbridge with handrail. It is reminiscent of the old washing place: and we even saw a resident wash her doormat. No dressing, but taking habits seriously – that's how it works.

TV This approach to lanes and squares by Burian took place through individual interventions. With the redesign of the exterior space around the castle and the Piarist church by Pleskot, this results in a whole – added together from contributions by changing authors, implemented in many steps over the course of 20 years.

FA Thanks to acupuncture within a "bigger" plan. This remains exciting, opens up potentials without completing, leaves fragments, allows development ...

TV ... provided it has power. Plečnik demonstrated as much – also with the opulence of his forms. These are hardly available to today's architects. Their work is more modest, even more direct – for example, the tub in front of Pleskot's museum entrance. Plecnik wanted to entertain pedestrians, to provide stimuli, images, stories. The same applies to Pleskot – his work is not abstract, I am being addressed.

FA The big fountain in the new monastery gardens by Babka, Květ, Sendler with the figurines by Zoubek should not be forgotten here. On hot

TV Schwierig. Künstlerische Direktheit? Jedenfalls schuf nur hier Johann Blasius Santini-Aichl starke Stimmung, indem er Gotik und Barock unakademisch mischte. Daran knüpft der tschechische Kubismus an, eine sehr eigene Ausprägung architektonischer Nationalromantik. Dann die konstruktivistische Architektur, die Zwischenkriegsmoderne, die hier viel expressiver und plastischer ausfällt als am Bauhaus. Beide Bewegungen berufen sich auf Plečnik. Plastizität, geistige Durchdringung der Körper – überspitzt gesagt: die Tschechen mögen's nicht flach. Das andere, das Bildhaft-Erzählerische, Freuden fürs Auge, auch da ist Plečnik Vorbild. Die Moderne der Zwischenkriegszeit sammelt sich in Tschechien unter dem Slogan: Poetismus. Da wirken surrealistische Strömungen, die sich im Untergrund bis zur Samtenen Revolution halten.

FA Plastisch und poetisch – ist das der Genius dieser Kultur?

TV Zusammen mit der Musik. Smetana kommt von hier. Man hört die Landschaft, die Weite, das Schwingen der Hügel, Wogen der Felder, Gurgeln des Wassers. Er schöpft aus der Volksmusik. Die Lieder der Menschen sind wie die Landschaft, sagt Rudolf Schwarz. Genius Loci – Ort lässt Landschaft spüren. Von den Türmen der Stadt sind die Felder zu sehen, die Vororte bleiben begrenzt. Möge das bleiben. Dann bleibt Litomyšl Vorbild.

days, it is very apparent how directly children pick up on things that are clearly present. Is this immediacy a key to our culture?

TV Hard to tell. Artistic directness? At any rate, this is the only place where Johann Blasius Santini-Aichl created a strong mood by mixing Gothic and baroque in a non-academic way. This was taken up by Czech cubism, a very distinctive characteristic of architectural national romanticism. Then constructivist architecture, the interwar modernism, which was much more expressive and sculptural here than that of the Bauhaus. Both movements refer to Plečnik. Plasticity and mental penetration of the body – to put it bluntly, the Czechs do not like it flat. The other, the pictorial-narrative, pleasures to the eye – here Plečnik is also a role model. Modernism of the interwar period in the Czech Republic rallied under the slogan of poetism. There were surrealistic tendencies there that were kept up underground until the Velvet Revolution.

FA Sculptural and poetic – is that the genius of this culture?

TV Together with the music. Smetana comes from here. You can hear the landscape, the vastness, the up and down of the hills, the billowing fields, the gurgling of the water. He drew from folk music. The songs of the people are like the landscape, says Rudolf Schwarz. Genius loci – a place makes its landscape palpable. From the towers of the town, the fields are visible, the suburbs remain limited. May that remain so. Then Litomyšl will remain exemplary.

Projekte

Projects

1
2
3
4
5
6
6
7
8
9
10
11
12
13
14
15
16
17
18
19
20

Der Schlossberg wird vom Renaissancebau (1568–1581) beherrscht. Die Renovierung der Sgraffiti durch Dissidenten-Künstler während der 1970-er bis 80er-Jahre prägte die Stadt einmal mehr.

The castle hill is dominated by the renaissance building (1568–1581). The renovation of the sgraffiti by dissident artists during the 1970s to 80s left an imprint on the city once again.

Feudale und sakrale Macht stehen dem bürgerlichen Gemeinwesen gegenüber. Die Hangkante mit Regionalmuseum, der Piaristenkirche und der Mauer des Klostergartens bildet eine natürliche Grenze.

Feudal and sacred power are situated opposite the civil community. The slope with the Regional Museum, the Piarist church and the monastery gardens' wall acts as a natural border.

Lageplan Schlossberg
Maßstab 1:5000
0 Schloss
1 Restauratorenschule
2 Ehemalige Schlossbrauerei
3 Regionalmuseum
4 Piaristenkirche
5 Piaristenkolleg
6 Reithalle und Remise

Site plan castle hill
Scale 1:5,000
0 Castle
1 Restoration School
2 Former castle brewery
3 Regional Museum
4 Piarist Church
5 Piarist college
6 Riding hall and carriage house

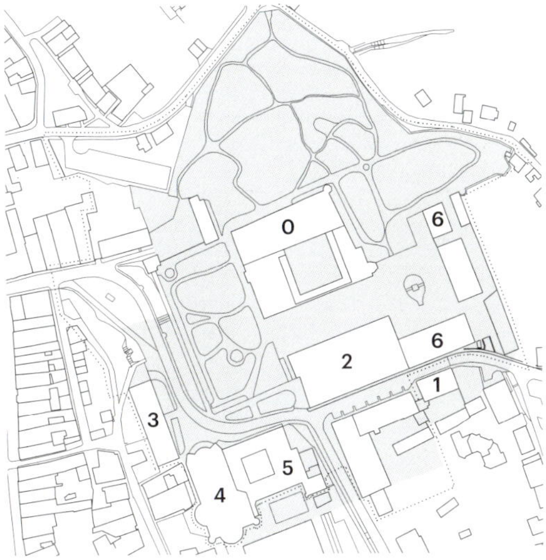

Schöpferisch bewahren

Creative Preservation

In einem kleinen Haus, das von Josef Váchal, Litomyšls erstem Künstlerdissidenten, ausgemalt ist, befindet sich heute ein Studio der Fakultät für Restaurierung der Universität von Pardubice. Nach der aufwendigen Sanierung der Fresken war die Idee einer privaten Schule aufgekommen, die später in der Universität aufging.
Die Stadt bot für den symbolischen Kaufpreis von einer Tschechischen Krone ein baufälliges Barockgebäude auf dem Schlossberg und setzte die Renovierung voraus. Der enge finanzielle Rahmen unterstützte die Absicht, Eingriffe auf ein Minimum zu beschränken. Im sanierten barocken Altbau entstanden Schulungsräume, Sanitäreinrichtungen und Gästewohnungen unter einem Dach. Der instand gesetzte Turm, Teil der mittelalterlichen Stadtmauer, schließt mit einer offenen Ausstellungs- und Aussichtsplattform ab. Ein Wirtschaftsgebäude beherbergt Ateliers und Labors mit neuer Belichtung über das verglaste Dach. Ein Neubau mit Atelier und Sanitärräumen aus Beton mit Sichtmauerwerk, Glas und Stahl schließt den intimen Schulhof mit dem stirnseitigen mittelalterlichen „Roten Turm" ab. Dessen offenes Satteldach mit Dachreiter, als Zimmermannskonstruktion ein Symbol handwerklichen Bauens, wurde gegen die Denkmalpflege erkämpft. Heute zählt er als beliebter Aussichtspunkt zu Litomyšls Wahrzeichen.

A small house whose interiors were painted by the first dissident artist of Litomyšl, Josef Váchal, now accommodates a studio of the Faculty of Restoration of the University of Pardubice. After elaborate renovation of the frescoes, the building was first supposed to be used by a private school, which then became part of the university.
The municipality provided a dilapidated baroque building on the castle hill for the symbolic price of a Czech crown, on condition that it be renovated. The tight financial framework supported the intention of limiting intervention to a minimum. Training rooms, sanitary facilities and guest flats were created under one roof in the renovated baroque building. The restored tower, part of the medieval town walls, has an open exhibition and observation platform at the top. A farm building houses studios and laboratories that enjoy new lighting from the glazed roof. A new building made of concrete with exposed masonry, glass and steel, containing a studio and sanitary facilities, and the medieval "Red Tower" at the front round off the intimate school yard. The tower's open gabled roof with a monitor – a carpenter's construction and thus a symbol of craftmanship – was negotiated against the monuments office's guidelines. Today it is a popular vantage point and one of Litomyšl's landmarks.

Architekt: Mikuláš Hulec, Eva Antošová, Prag
Bauherr: Stadt Litomyšl, Universität Pardubice
Kategorie: Umbau und Sanierung Kultureinrichtung
Planung: 1992–1997
Ausführung: 1993–1998
Adresse: Jiráskova 3

Architects: Mikuláš Hulec, Eva Antošová, Prague
Clients: Municipality of Litomyšl, University of Pardubice
Category: Alteration and renovation, cultural facility
Planning: 1992–1997
Construction: 1993–1998
Address: Jiráskova 3

Grundriss
Maßstab 1:400
1 Altbau, Unterrichtsräume
2 Roter Turm, Ausstellung
3 Nebengebäude, Wirtschaftsgebäude Ateliers, Labors
4 Neubau

Floor plan
Scale 1:400
1 Old building, classrooms
2 Red Tower, exhibition
3 Former farm building, studios
4 New building, laboratories

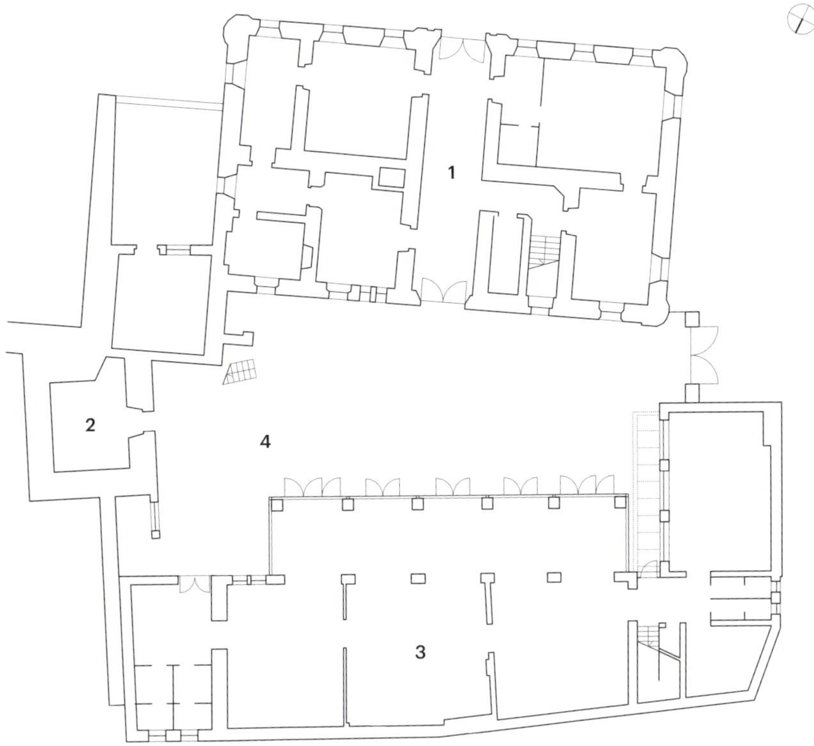

Neue Gäste im ehemaligen Brauhaus

New Guests in the Former Brewery

Ursprünglich aus der Renaissance erhielt das Gebäude sein wesentliches Aussehen im Barock und wurde im 19. Jahrhundert zur Industrieanlage umgebaut. In einem Wohnbereich wurde 1824 Bedřich Smetana geboren. Den Verfall nach 1945 beendete 2000 die Entscheidung für eine städtische Nutzung und die Einrichtung eines Schulungszentrums des Christlichen Vereins Junger Menschen (CVJM).
In mehreren Abschnitten und über Jahre wurde umgebaut, wobei die Fassade zum Hauptplatz und Räume für ein Tourismusbüro den Anfang machten. Unterkünfte und Seminarräume für den CVJM sowie Sonderräume folgten.
Restaurierung, Umnutzung und Umbau unterlagen der Prämisse, alle historischen Stadien, auch unserer Zeit, sichtbar werden zu lassen und den Charakter eines Funktionsbaus zu betonen. Weder Anpassung noch gesuchten Kontrast fordert Pleskot, sondern: intakte Strukturen nutzen, Alt und Neu in ein angemessenes Verhältnis setzen statt zu homogenisieren, neue Elemente unaufgeregt einsetzen, die Umgebung durch den Umbau stärken. Historische Bausubstanz steht neben industriell Vorgefertigtem, Ziegel, Kalk, Naturstein, offener Holz-Dachstuhl neben rohem Stahl, Beton, Spanplatten, Kunststoffe und eine offene Installation. Hervorzuheben ist die raffinierte Lichtführung ohne durchgehende Helligkeit. Entschiedener Zugriff statt exzessiver Perfektion macht den Umbau zum Erlebnis. Die Platzgestaltung vor dem Komplex ist der letzte Bauabschnitt.

Originally from the Renaissance, the building was given its essential appearance in the baroque period and was rebuilt in the 19th century to house an industrial plant. Bedřich Smetana was born in one of its living quarters in 1824. The building's decay after 1945 ended in 2000 when a decision was made to repurpose it for a municipal use and for a training centre of the Christian Association of Young People (YMCA).
It was rebuilt in several sections and over several years, beginning with the facade towards the main square and with premises for a tourist office. Accommodations and seminar rooms for the YMCA as well as special rooms followed.
Restoration, conversion and reconstruction were subject to the premise that all historical stages, including our current time, become visible and that the building's functional nature be emphasised. Pleskot's aim was neither to adapt nor to look for contrast, but to use intact structures, put old and new in an appropriate relationship instead of homogenising, install new elements in a matter-of-fact way and to use the conversion to bolster the surroundings. Historical structures are now next to industrially prefabricated elements, brick, lime, natural stone and an open timber roof truss next to raw steel, concrete, particle board, plastics and unenclosed installations. The building's sophisticated lighting without continuous brightness is a remarkable aspect. Decided intervention instead of excessive perfection has turned the alteration into an experience. The redesign of the square in front of the complex will form the final construction phase.

Architekt: Josef Pleskot / AP atelier, Prag
Bauherr: Stadt Litomyšl, Europäische Allianz YMCA
Kategorie: Umbau und Sanierung Kultureinrichtung
Planung: 2001, 2007–2008
Ausführung: 2001–2006, 2011–2014
Adresse: Jiráskova 133

Architect: Josef Pleskot / AP atelier, Prague
Client: Municipality of Litomyšl, European Alliance of YMCAs
Category: Alteration and renovation, cultural facility
Planning: 2001, 2007–2008
Construction: 2001–2006, 2011–2014
Address: Jiráskova 133

Schnitt / Grundriss
Maßstab 1:750
1 Tourismusbüro
2 Durchgang zum Schloss
3 interner Hof
4 ökumenische Kapelle
5 Durchgang
6 Ausstellungshallen
7 Aufgang zu Gästeräumen

Section / Floor plan
Scale 1:750
1 Tourist office
2 Access to castle
3 Internal courtyard
4 Ecumenical chapel
5 Passageway
6 Exhibition halls
7 Stairs to guest rooms

aa

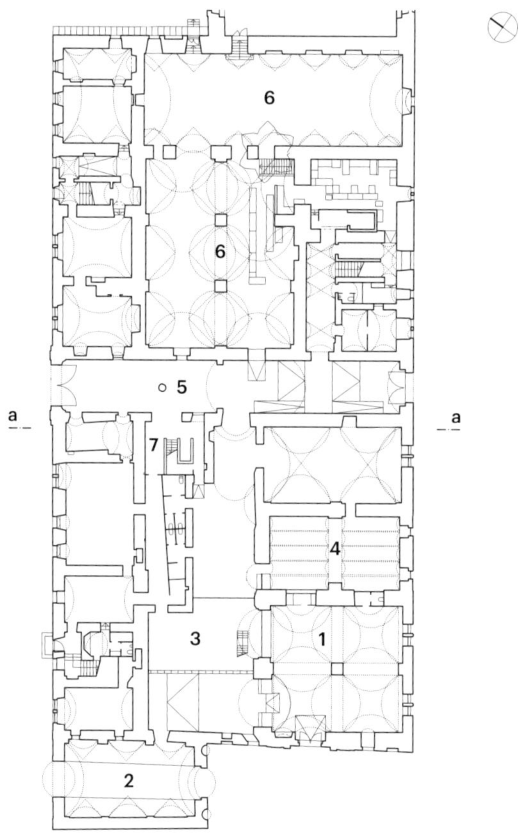

Bildung gestern und heute

Education Yesterday and Today

Einst Schulgebäude der Piaristen beherbergt der barocke Block mit neuem Zeltdach seit 1926 das Regionalmuseum. Der Bau grenzt den Bereich kirchlicher und politischer Macht auf dem Schlossberg von der tiefergelegenen Bürgerstadt ab. Ausgrabungen vor dem Gebäude veranlassten 2012 die Verlegung des Eingangs und die Sicherung von Funden aus der frühen Stadtgeschichte. Die Längserschließung des Gebäudes erfolgt nun durch einen vorgelagerten Kopfbau, die Funde bleiben unterirdisch sichtbar. Beide Bereiche sind pyramidal abgedeckt – die unterirdischen Räume durch flachgeneigte Pflasterflächen des Platzes, der Kopfbau durch ein asymmetrisches Metalldach. Der Bau für Empfang und Museumsshop verbirgt sich hinter einer niedrigen Barockwand. Dem Eingang rückseitig entgegengesetzt eröffnet eine raumhohe Glaswand, um 45° eingedreht, unverstellte Blicke über die Stadt. Darunter verbindet eine Treppenanlage die Ober- mit der Unterstadt. Die neue Raumfolge wird zweimal durch senkrecht angeordnete Treppen unterbrochen, die das Museum mit der Stadt bzw. der vorgelagerten Terrasse des Museumscafés verbinden.
Der schlichte Barockbau hat einen neuen Auftritt; dreiseitig ist er durch pyramidenartige Volumen aus dem Alltagsbauen herausgehoben.

Once a Piarist school building, the baroque block with a new tented roof has housed the Regional Museum since 1926. The building separates the area of ecclesiastical and political power on the castle hill from the civil town below.
Excavations in front of the building in 2012 prompted the relocation of the entrance and the securing of finds from the town's early history. The building is now accessed through a new building attached to its end, while the finds remain visible underground. Both areas are covered by pyramidal structures – the underground spaces by flat-inclined paved areas on the square, the building at the end by an asymmetrical metal roof. This building containing the reception and museum shop is partly hidden behind a low baroque wall. Opposite to the entrance, towards the rear of the building, a room-high glass wall rotated by 45° provides unobstructed views over the town. Underneath, a staircase connects the upper and lower town.
The new sequence of rooms is interrupted twice by perpendicular staircases that connect the museum with the town and with the terrace in front of the museum café, respectively.
The simple baroque building has a new setting; thanks to pyramidal volumes on three sides, it is made to contrast with everyday building products.

Architekt: Josef Pleskot / AP atelier, Prag
Bauherr: Region Pardubice
Kategorie: Umbau und Sanierung Kultureinrichtung
Planung: 2007
Ausführung: 2012–2014
Adresse: Jiráskova 9

Architect: Josef Pleskot / AP atelier, Prague
Client: Region of Pardubice
Category: Alteration and renovation, cultural facility
Planning: 2007
Construction: 2012–2014
Address: Jiráskova 9

Grundriss / Schnitte
Maßstab 1:750
1 Eingang
2 Ausstellung
3 Ausstellung, Café
4 Freisitz Café

Floor plan / Sections
1 Entrance
2 Exhibition
3 Café
4 Café terrace

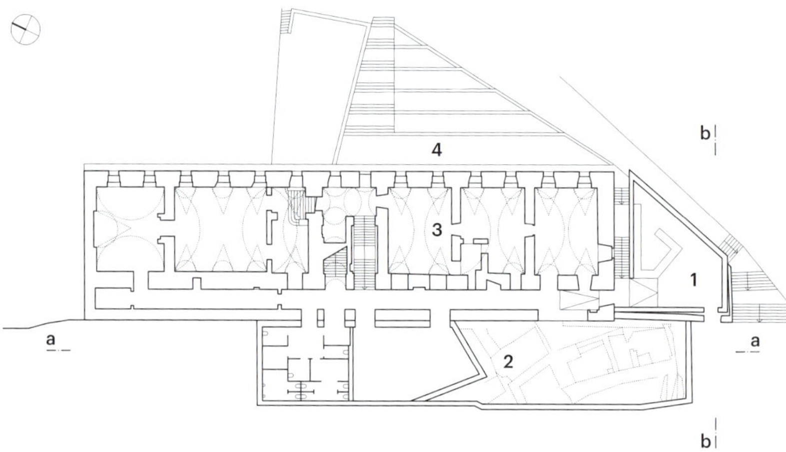

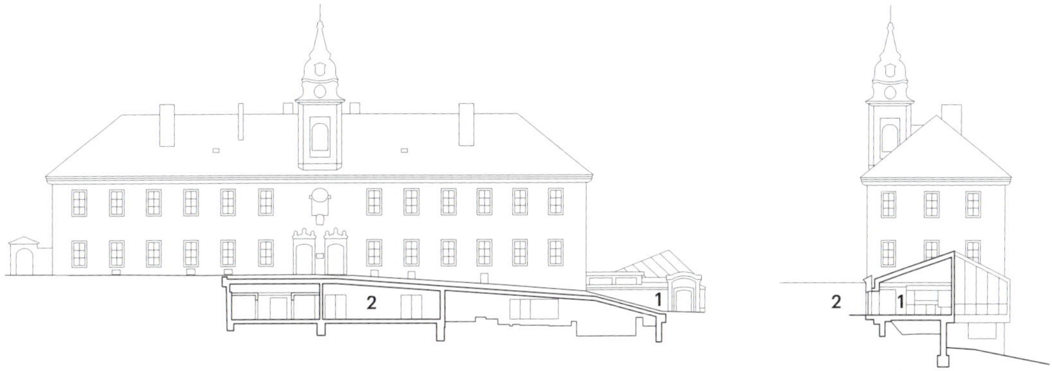

aa bb

Wiedergeburt eines Wahrzeichens

Rebirth of a Landmark

Die 1722 fertiggestellte Barockkirche nach dem Entwurf von Giovanni Battista Alliprandi war Hauskirche des Piaristenklosters, das 1948 aufgelöst wurde. Heute ist der Sakralbau die weithin sichtbare Dominante der Stadt. Nach 1945 begann der Niedergang, bis zur Verwendung als Autogarage und großer Zerstörung im Inneren. Seit 1972 in Staatsbesitz begann 2007 im Zusammenhang mit der Erneuerung des Schlosshügels die Wiederherstellung der Kirche und ihre Rückführung an den Orden. Neben sakralen Aufgaben dient sie seit 2014 schulischen, kulturellen und touristischen Zwecken.

Die Erneuerung thematisiert die turbulente Geschichte, die erlebbar bleibt. Der große Innenraum wird durch helle Grautöne akzentuiert, die zurückhaltende Ausstattung ist sorgfältig restauriert. Neue Einbauten, so die Bänke des Nebenschiffs und ein neuer Volksaltar, geben sich als zeitgenössisch zu erkennen. Das gilt auch für eine Brücke aus Holz und Stahl, die einen Rundgang auf der Ebene der Emporen erlaubt – heute auch ein Ort für Ausstellungen. Künstlerische Interventionen wie Jahreszahlen im Boden oder eine Licht-Glas-Installation in der Vierung betonen den Zeitbezug. Die Treppe zur Aussichtsplattform zwischen den Türmen macht erstmals ein seltenes Höhenerlebnis öffentlich zugänglich.

The baroque church, designed by Giovanni Battista Alliprandi and completed in 1722, belonged to the Piarist monastery, which was dissolved in 1948. Visible from afar, the sacred building is the dominant feature of the town today. After 1945, it went into decay, culminating in its use as a garage and heavy damage to its interior. Having been in state ownership since 1972, the restoration of the church and its return to the Piarist order was taken up in 2007 in connection with the castle hill renovations. Since 2014, in addition to sacred duties, it has been serving school, cultural and tourist purposes.

The renewal addresses the building's turbulent history and makes it palpable. The large interior has been accented by light shades of gray, the restrained features have been carefully restored. New installations, such as the benches in the side nave and a new people's altar, are visibly contemporary. This also applies to a bridge made of wood and steel, which allows a round tour on the level of the choir galleries – today also a place for exhibitions. Artistic interventions such as year dates in the ground or a light-glass installation in the crossing emphasise the reference of time. A staircase to the viewing platform between the towers has made this rare experience of altitude publicly accessible for the first time.

Architekt: Atelier Štěpán, Marek Štěpán, Vanda Štěpánova, Brünn
Bauherr: Stadt Litomyšl
Kategorie: Umbau Sanierung Sakralbau
Planung: 2007–2011
Ausführung: 2011–2014
Adresse: Jiráskova

Architects: Atelier Štěpán, Marek Štěpán, Vanda Štěpánova, Brno
Client: Municipality of Litomyšl
Category: Alteration and renovation, sacred building
Planning: 2007–2011
Construction: 2011–2014
Address: Jiráskova

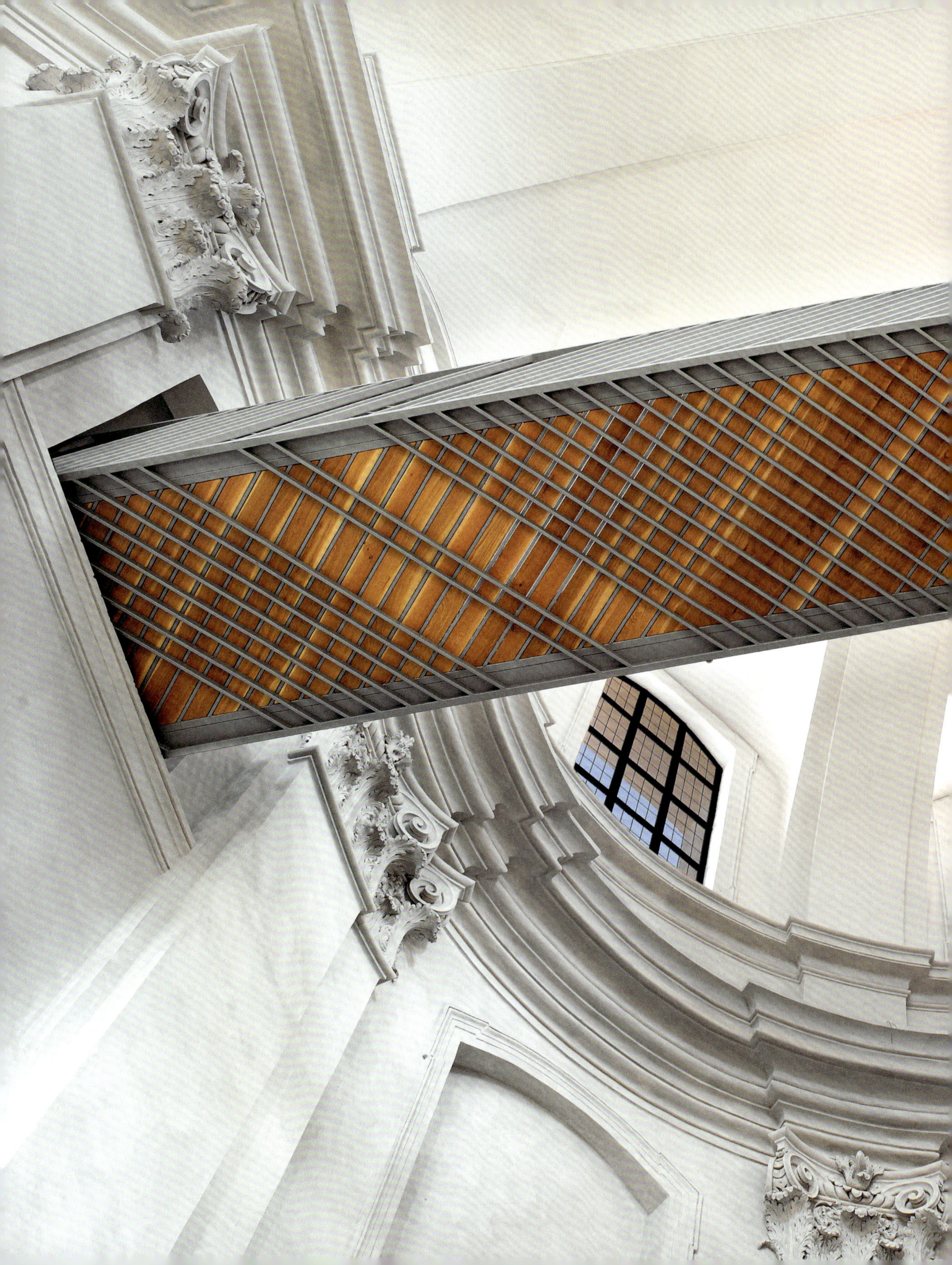

Schnitt / Grundriss
Maßstab 1:750

1 Ergänzung Empore
2 Türme mit Aussichtsplattform
3 Zugang zur Krypta

Section / Floor plan
Scale 1:750

1 Gallery extension
2 Towers with viewing platform
3 Entrance to crypt

aa

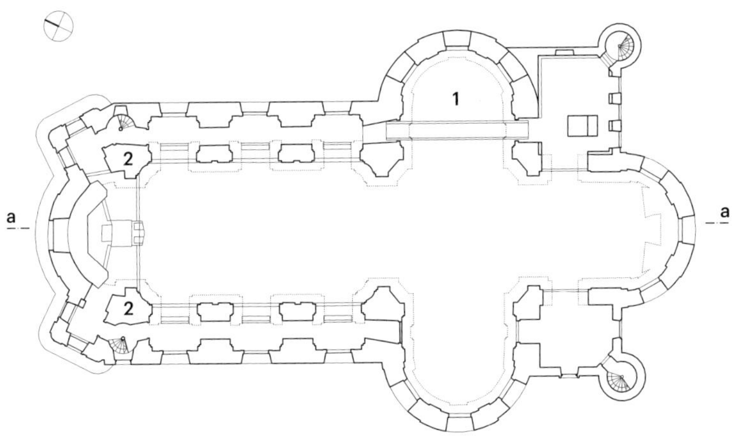

Emporenebene /
Gallery level

Räume des Wissens

Chambers of Learning

Ende des 17. Jahrhunderts entstand das Kloster der Piaristen für Wohn- und Versammlungszwecke um einen Kreuzgang. Erst ein halbes Jahrhundert später folgte das Gotteshaus. Der Tradition des Ordens folgend wird heute wieder gewohnt und unterrichtet: Die Fakultät für Restaurierung (Papier, Buch, Buch und Stein) der Universität von Pardubice hat hier ihren Hauptsitz.
Die alten Gemäuer wurden unter Beibehaltung der Raumschale in heutigen Standard versetzt und neue Bezüge zum rückwärtigen Klostergarten geöffnet.
Östlich schließt ein Neubau für Bibliothek und Festsaal an. Er folgt dem Bestand in Geschoss- und Traufhöhe, betont aber mit Flachdach und geschosshoher Verglasung nach Norden sachlich zurückhaltend Eigenständigkeit. Das geschlämmte Mauerwerk seiner Wände ist Bezug zum Bestand. Der freie Blick aus der Präsenzbibliothek schafft eine besondere Beziehung – das Schloss ist vierte Wand. Der weite Raum mit einer Galerie aus Stahl und Holz für frei zugängliche Regale und Leseplätze lebt von der filigranen Konstruktion mit sinnfälligen, sprechenden Details. Der Raum darunter dient Versammlungen der Universität oder der Gemeinde und lässt sich zum vorgelegten Hof mit zum Platz ansteigenden Sitzstufen öffnen.

In the late 17th century, the Piarist monastery built rooms for residential and congregational purposes around a cloister. The church was only erected half a century later. Following the order's tradition, the college building is now used for living and teaching again: the University of Pardubice's Faculty of Restoration (paper, book, book and stone) is now based here.
While maintaining the spatial envelope, the old walls were reworked to meet today's standards, and new visual links with the monastery gardens in the rear were opened.
A new building with a library and a ceremonial hall was attached in the east. It has the same storey and eaves height as the existing building, but the flat roof and storey-high glazing to the north are evidence of its discreetly functional indepencence. The lime-washed masonry of its walls refers to the existing building. The unimpeded view from the reference library creates a special relationship – the castle acts as a fourth wall. The wide space with a gallery of steel and wood for freely accessible shelves and reading places draws its power from the filigree construction with meaningful and obvious details. The room below serves for university or community gatherings and can be opened to the courtyard, with seating steps ascending towards the square.

Architekt: Architektonická kancelář Burian – Křivinka, Aleš Burian, Gustav Křivinka, Brünn
Bauherr: Stadt Litomyšl
Kategorie: Umbau, Sanierung und Neubau Bildungseinrichtungen
Planung: 2008
Ausführung: 2011–2015
Adresse: Jiráskova 8

Architects: Architektonická kancelář Burian – Křivinka, Aleš Burian, Gustav Křivinka, Brno
Client: Municipality of Litomyšl
Category: Alteration, renovation and new building, education facilities
Planning: 2008
Construction: 2011–2015
Address: Jiráskova 8

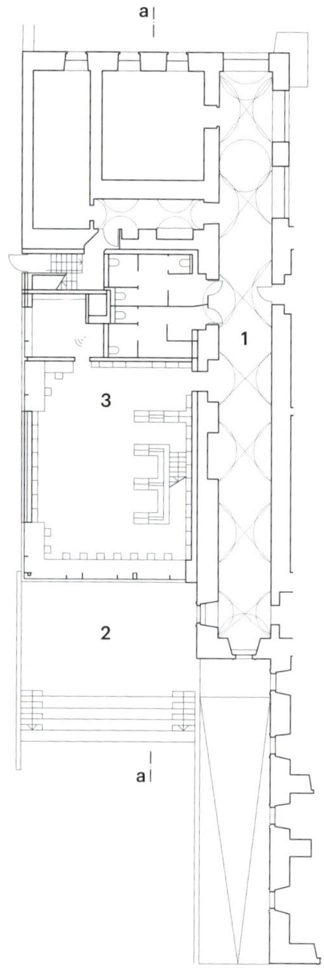

Grundriss / Schnitt
Maßstab 1:400
1 Kreuzgang
2 Hof mit Freitreppe
3 Bibliothek
4 Auditorium
5 Dachgarten

Floor plan / Section
Scale 1:400
1 Cloister
2 Courtyard with seating steps
3 Library
4 Auditorium
5 Roof garden

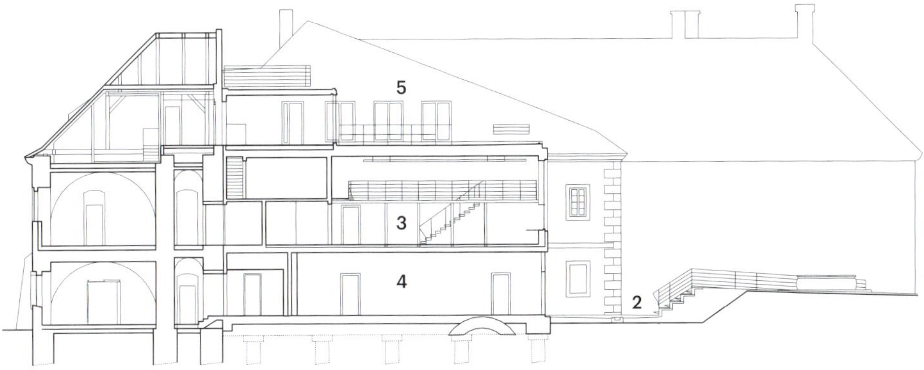

aa

Kunststoff im Barock

Plastic in the Baroque

Barocke Zweckbauten begrenzen den oberen Schlosshof – darunter eine kleine Wagenremise und eine große Reithalle. Aus dem fortgeschrittenen Verfall folgte der radikale Zugriff für neue Nutzung. Die Bauten, neu bedacht, verhalten sich zur historischen Form abstrakt. Die Reithalle ist heute Veranstaltungshalle, mit feinem Oberflächenrelief als Architekturschmuck. Die Remise beherbergt heute ein Café und Büros und besticht durch den Rhythmus der Öffnungen in der Wand.
Die Einrichtung löst sich von der Hülle. Wechselnutzung, Akustik und Technik des Veranstaltungsraums werden auf unkonventionelle Art bewältigt. Einem feststehenden Einbau für Künstlerräume steht eine formschlüssige Schale gegenüber – die Bühne, die auf Schienen bewegt werden kann und Platz nach Bedarf einräumt. Beides sind Schalen aus Laminat, leicht und akustisch wirksam. Aus gleichem Stoff ist der Boden, einfachst zur ansteigenden Ebene zu verwandeln. Weitere Technik ist in einer variablen Decke abgehängt.
Die Einrichtung des nur verputzten Cafés addiert sich aus festen Tisch-Bank-Einheiten, gegossen aus glasfaserverstärktem Kunstoff (GFK). Konzeptionell und stofflich folgen dem alle Einbauten. Radikal der Stoff – durchscheinendes Laminat, industriell-roh, im Ton passend – und seine totale Anwendung.

Baroque functional buildings surround the upper castle courtyard – among them a small carriage house and a large riding hall. Advanced decay led to a radical intervention for new uses. The reconsidered buildings are an abstraction of the historical form. The riding hall has been turned into an event hall, with a fine surface relief as architectural decoration. The carriage house, which now contains a café and offices, impresses with the rhythm of the openings in its facade.
The interior is detached from the shell. The changing uses, acoustics and technology of the event space are handled in an unconventional way. A fixed installation for artists' rooms stands opposite the form-fitting shell of the stage, which can be moved on rails and provides space as needed. Both are lightweight and acoustically effective laminate shells. The floor is of the same material, easy to transform into a rising level. Additional technology is hidden in a variable suspended ceiling.
The furnishings of the plastered café consist of fixed table-bench units also cast in laminate. Conceptually and materially, all furnishings follow this example. A radical fabric – translucent laminate, industrial and raw, in a matching tone – and its total application.

Architekt: HŠH Architekti, Tomáš Hradečný, Jan Šépka, Petr Hájek, Prag
Bauherr: Stadt Litomyšl
Kategorie: Umbau und Sanierung Kultur und Freizeit
Planung: 2007–10
Ausführung: 2011–2014
Adresse: Jiráskova

Architects: HŠH Architects, Tomáš Hradečný, Jan Šépka, Petr Hájek, Prague
Client: Municipality of Litomyšl
Category: Alteration and renovation, cultural and leisure facilities
Planning: 2007–10
Construction: 2011–2014
Address: Jiráskova

Grundriss / Schnitt
Maßstab 1:400

1 Veranstaltungssaal, Ausstellungshalle
2 Bühne
3 Technik, WC

Floor plan / Section
Scale 1:400

1 Event hall, exhibition hall
2 Stage
3 Building services, WC

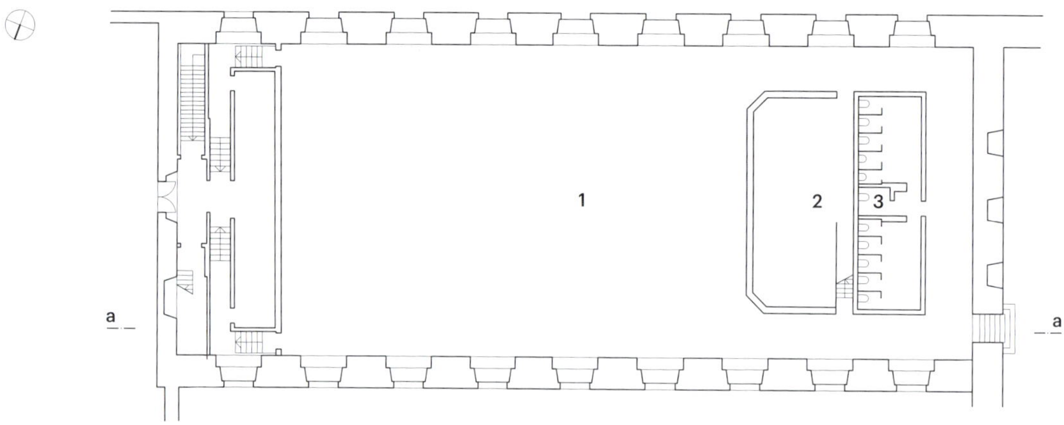

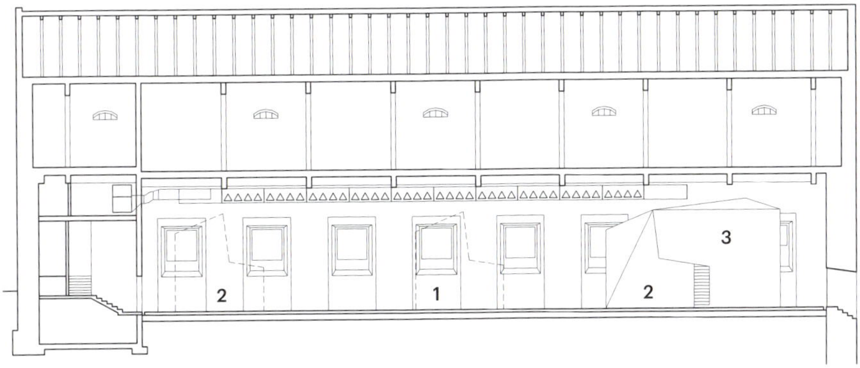

aa

Schnitt / Grundriss
Maßstab 1:400
1 Café
2 Bar
3 Nebenräume und Erschließung
4 Büroräume

Section / Floor plan
Scale 1:400
1 Café
2 Bar
3 Ancillary rooms and circulation
4 Offices

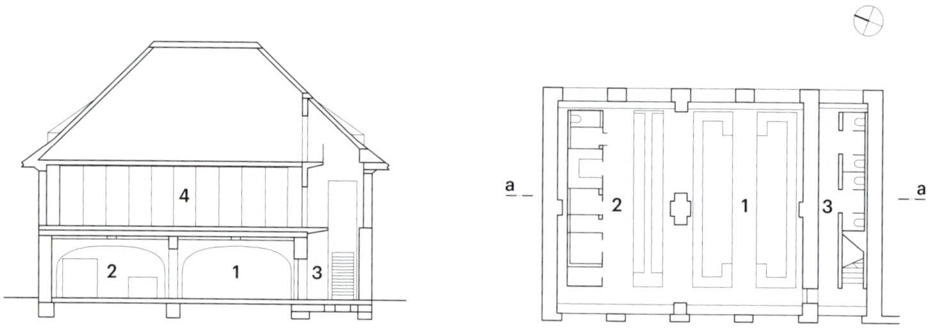

aa

Beiläufigkeit von Platz und Weg

Squares and Paths as a Matter of Course

Abseits des großen Stadtplatzes, unterhalb des Schlossbergs, liegt der älteste Teil der Stadt mit der ehemaligen Spitalkirche im Zentrum und der gotischen Dekanatskirche. Enge Gassen wechseln hier mit übersichtlichen Plätzen. Mit der Neugestaltung dieser urbanen Räume ab 1996 begannen der Rückbau des Asphaltdschungels und die Wiedergewinnung von städtischem Charakter, Ordnung und Struktur.

Der Verkehr wurde reduziert und Flächen gepflastert, wo möglich mit vorhandenem Material niedrigschwellig abgesetzt, differenziert in Pflastergröße und Verlegemuster. So ergeben sich Linien, die Orientierung bieten, zum Bestand vermitteln und Plätze fassen. Wenige Objekte wie Poller aus Granit oder Gusseisen, Papierkörbe oder feste Bänke genügen, um dies zu unterstreichen. Ein kleiner Trinkbrunnen zentriert den Platz vor der Spitalkirche. Selbstverständlich fasst die einstige Reitertreppe mit neuem Geländer in weitem Schwung, von alten Baumkronen bedacht, den Raum vor der Dekanatskirche. Dezentes Spiel der Pflasterung, zurückhaltende Möblierung, einfache geometrische Figuren und Einbeziehung alten Baumbestandes in neue Ordnungen verleihen dieser Raumfolge beiläufigen Charakter – als wär's seit jeher so.

Away from the large town square, below the castle hill, is the oldest part of the town, with the former hospital church in the centre and the Gothic Dean's Church. Narrow lanes alternate with little squares here. The redesign of these urban spaces from 1996 on was a first step towards clearing the asphalt jungle and recovering urban character, order and structure.

Traffic was reduced and surfaces were paved using existing material where possible, off-set with a low threshold and differentiated by stone size and laying pattern. This results in lines that provide orientation, create transitions towards existing buildings and form a frame for squares. Just a few objects such as granite or cast-iron bollards, wastebaskets or fixed benches are all that is needed for accenting. A small drinking fountain gives the square in front of the hospital church a centre. The wide sweep of the former equestrian staircase with a new banister and roofed by old treetops forms a natural frame for the space in front of the Dean's Church. The subtle play of the paving, restrained furnishing, simple geometric figures and the inclusion of old trees in new orders give this sequence of spaces an incidental character – as if it had been like this forever.

Architekt: Architektonická kancelář Burian – Křivinka, Aleš Burian, Gustav Křivinka, Brünn
Bauherr: Stadt Litomyšl
Kategorie: Sanierung Öffentlicher Raum
Planung: 1996–2000, 2007
Ausführung: 1996–2007
Adresse: Touloucovo; Šantovo

Architects: Architektonická kancelář Burian – Křivinka, Aleš Burian, Gustav Křivinka, Brno
Client: Municipality of Litomyšl
Category: Renovation, public space
Planning: 1996–2000, 2007
Construction: 1996–2007
Address: Touloucovo; Šantovo

Lageplan
Maßstab 1:1500

Site plan
Scale 1:1,500

1 Toulovcovo-Platz mit Spitalkirche
2 Santovo Platz mit Dekanatskirche
3 Ruzova-Gasse
4 Hotel Aplaus

1 Toulovcovo Square with Hospital Church
2 Santovo Square with Dean's Church
3 Ruzova Lane
4 Hotel Aplaus

Der grüne Balkon der Stadt

The Town's Green Balcony

Bis zur Auflösung des Piaristenklosters 1948 war der Klostergarten bewirtschaftet. Im Anschluss verfiel er ebenso wie der ehemalige, 1,1 ha große Friedhof. 1997 beschloss der Stadtrat, diesen Bereich zu revitalisieren. Der aus einem Wettbewerb hervorgegangene Entwurf stand unter dem Motto: „Garten-Theater, Theater-Garten" und knüpfte an die Ordnung und das Konzept der freien Sicht von Renaissancegärten an.
Der weite Horizont schließt die beiden Hauptkirchen der Stadt als Dominanten an seinen Rändern ein, die einen feinen Richtungswechsel der Wege, Mäuerchen und offenen Rasenflächen ergeben. In deren Schnittpunkt liegt eine große Wasserfläche mit lebhaften Figuren des Bildhauers Olbram Zoubek. Das leicht geneigte Terrain verschafft Überblick mit der Silhouette der Stadt als Kulisse. Zu den Rändern liegen herausgehobene Bereiche wie ein Kräutergarten als Freisitz der Cafeteria der angrenzenden Hochschule, ein Aussichtspavillon, Blumenrabatten an der Grenzmauer. Die freie Mitte wird durch wenige Bäume, Reminiszenzen an den alten Garten, eher betont.
Seit 2000 besitzt Litomyšl nun einen zentralen, öffentlichen Park, ein kräftiger Impuls für Bürgervertrauen in Stadtgestaltung. Der belebte Park zählt unter die besten öffentlichen Plätze des Landes seit 1990.

The monastery gardens had been farmed until the dissolution of the Piarist monastery in 1948. Afterwards, they fell into disuse just like the former 1.1 ha large cemetery. In 1997, the town council decided to revitalise the area. The design resulting from the subsequent competition had the guiding principle of "Garden Theatre, Theatre Garden" and it followed the order and concept of the unimpeded views in Renaissance gardens.
The wide horizon includes the town's two main churches as dominants on its edges, which result in a subtle change of direction of the paths, low walls and open lawns. At their intersection lies a large expanse of water with lively figurines by the sculptor Olbram Zoubek. The slightly sloping terrain provides an overview, with the town's silhouette forming the backdrop. Towards the edges are more elaborated areas such as a herb garden forming a terrace for the cafeteria of the adjacent college, a viewing pavilion, and flower borders at the boundary wall. The void in the centre is accentuated by a few trees reminiscent of the old gardens.
This central, public park in Litomyšl has now been a powerful impetus for citizen confidence in urban development since 2000. The lively park is one of the country's best public spaces after the Velvet Revolution.

Architekt: Václav Babka, Radko Květ, Zdeněk Sendler, Brünn
Bauherr: Stadt Litomyšl
Kategorie: Erschließung und Sanierung Öffentlicher Raum
Planung: 1997–1998
Ausführung: 1999–2000
Adresse: Zámecká

Architects: Václav Babka, Radko Květ, Zdeněk Sendler, Brno
Client: Municipality of Litomyšl
Category: Development and renovation, public space
Planning: 1997–1998
Construction: 1999–2000
Address: Zámecká

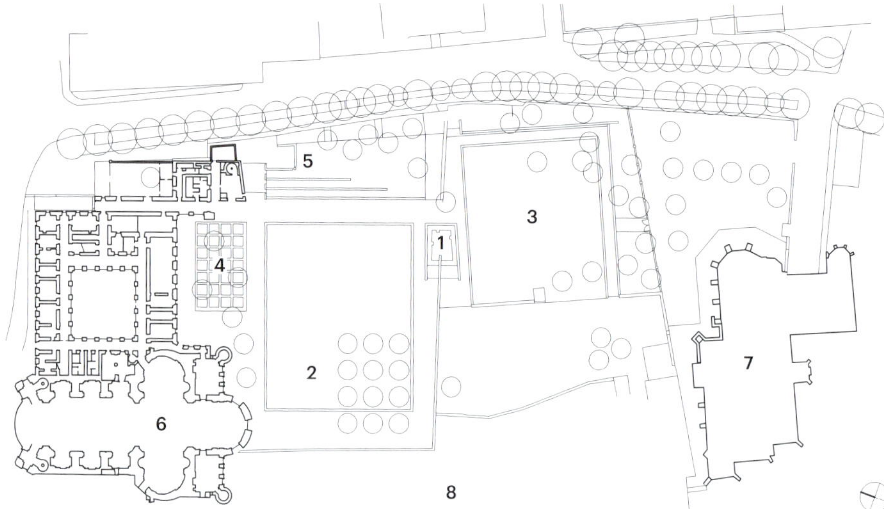
5
3
1
4
2
7
6
8

Lageplan
Maßstab 1:2000
1 Brunnen
2 ehemaliger Klostergarten
3 ehemaliger Dekanatsgarten, Friedhof
4 Kräutergarten
5 Pavillon
6 Piaristenkirche, Kolleg
7 Dekanatskirche
8 Bürgerstadt

Site plan
Scale 1:2,000
1 Fountain
2 Former monastery gardens
3 Former deanery garden, cemetery
4 Herb garden
5 Pavilion
6 Piarist Church, college
7 Dean's Church
8 Civil town

Aus dem Dornröschenschlaf erwacht

Awakened from a Deep Slumber

Der Flusslauf der Loučná, einst westliche Begrenzung der Altstadt, verwahrloste mit dem Ende der Wasserkraftnutzung und dem Bau der barriereartigen Durchgangsstraße. Heftige Überschwemmungen zwangen 2001 zur Planung eines neuen Hochwasserschutzes.
Der neue Ansatz des 1. Bauabschnitts: Bester Schutz ist städtische Nutzung – das vernachlässigte Gerinnsel wird zum belebten Stadtraum; hier begegnen sich Natur und gebaute Kultur. Einem naturbelassenen Ufer liegt ein geradliniger befestigter Fußweg gegenüber. Breite Abtreppungen vermitteln vom Fluss zur höher gelegenen Promenade. Zusätzlich zu den bestehenden Brücken kommt eine Holzplattform, die die Ufer verbindet und einen Platz über dem Fluss schafft. Sparsame, doch im Detail kräftige Interventionen stehen „wilder" Natur gegenüber.
Zwölf Jahre später folgt der 2. Bauabschnitt flussaufwärts: Nun sind beide Ufer intensiv und verspielt bearbeitet, der Umgriff deutlich erweitert. Stadtseitig sind Straße, Wiesenstreifen und Ufer zu einem öffentlichen Raum zusammengefasst, ein Kinderspielplatz mit künstlerischen Objekten für Groß und Klein lockt. Als Rückgrat fungiert ein geknickter roter Betonbalken, Sitzplatz und Uferbefestigung zugleich. Hängebrücke und Steinfurt führen zum anderen Ufer mit neuem, gedecktem Festplatz vor dem Volkshaus, dazu ein Aussichtsturm.

The course of the River Loučná, once the western boundary of the Old Town, had been neglected with the end of the use of hydroelectric power and the construction of the barrier-like through-road. Heavy floods in 2001 necessitated the planning of a new flood protection.
The new approach of the 1st construction phase: urban use is the best form of protection, the neglected rivulet becomes an animated urban space; nature and built culture meet. A natural bank is faced by a straight, paved footpath on the other. Wide stepped structures create a transition between the river and the promenade above. In addition to the existing bridges, there is a wooden platform that connects the banks and creates a square above the river. Sparing but powerful interventions in terms of detail are opposite "wild" nature here.
Twelve years later, the second construction phase followed a little upstream: now both banks have had intensive and playful worked done and the transformation has been extended significantly. On the town side, the street, green areas and banks have been combined into a public space, and a children's playground with artistic objects for young and old forms a new attraction. The development's backbone is presented by a kinked red concrete beam that acts as seating and river-bank reinforcement at the same time. A suspension bridge and stepping stones lead to the other bank with a new, covered fairground in front of the Community Hall, including a lookout tower.

Architekt 1. BA: Josef Pleskot / AP atelier, Prag
Architekt 2. BA: Rusina Frei architekti,
Martin Rusina, Martin Frei, Prag
Bauherr: Stadt Litomyšl
Planung: 2001, 2013–2015
Ausführung: 2001–2002, 2016–2017
Kategorie: Sanierung und Erschließung Öffentlicher Raum
Adresse: Vodní Valy, Bernardka

Architects 1st phase: Josef Pleskot / AP atelier, Prague
Architects 2nd phase: Rusina Frei architekti,
Martin Rusina, Martin Frei, Prague
Client: Municipality of Litomyšl
Planning: 2001, 2013–2015
Construction: 2001–2002, 2016–2017
Category: Renovation and development, public space
Address: Vodní Valy, Bernardka

Lageplan
Maßstab 1:4000

1 Ufergestaltung Pleskot AP atelier
2 Ufergestaltung Rusina, Frei

3 Bastionsbrücke
4 Platzbrücke
5 Treppenanlage
6 Spielplatz
7 Hängebrücke
8 Pavillon Freisitz Smetana-Haus
9 Aussichtspunkt
10 Furt

11 Smetana-Haus
12 Komenski-Platz und Denkmal
13 Plattenbauten
14 Stadtplatz

Site plan
Scale 1:4,000

1 Riverbanks by Pleskot AP atelier
2 Riverbanks by Rusina, Frei

3 Bastion Bridge
4 Square above river
5 Stepped structures
6 Playground
7 Suspended bridge
8 Pavilion and outdoor seating, Smetana House
9 Viewpoint
10 Stepping stones

11 Smetana House
12 Komenski Square and memorial
13 Prefab buildings ("Plattenbau")
14 Main square

Natur und Geometrie

Nature and Geometry

Anlässlich des hundertjährigen Bestehens der Pädagogischen Hochschule wurde der rückwärtige Hof der Schule von einem Parkplatz in einen Ort der Ruhe und Erholung verwandelt. Der neue Platz bezieht sich auf die umgebende Architektur der Neorenaissance, entfaltet ein Spiel strenger Geometrie, belebt durch differenziertes Grün und das Plätschern eines Brunnens.
Dieser bildet die Mitte des Hofes, steht in der Achse des Schulgebäudes und gibt den Ton an: Ein Würfel aus rohem Stahl mit senkrechten Schlitzen, die reichlich Wasser freigeben, steht im Zentrum eines quadratischen Rostes, der das Wasser schluckt. Die angrenzende Fläche zum Schulbau ist mit geometrisch rhythmisiertem Granit gepflastert. Gegenüber liegt eine quadratische Rasenfläche, begrenzt durch Hainbuchen, in der Diagonale steht eine Linde. Zum seitlich vorbeiführenden Fußweg erhebt sich eine mannshohe Struktur – weniger Zaun denn endloses Metallband, das im Vorübergehen changiert. Zum seitlichen Nachbarn schließt eine Pergola an mit rankenden Rosen und Bänken, ergänzt um feste und bewegliche, geometrisch strenge Sitzgelegenheiten auf dem Hof. Ein Kabinettstück an Ausgewogenheit, sei es von Kultur und Natur oder von Geometrie und Zufall.

On the occasion of the College of Education's centennial, the courtyard behind the school was transformed from a parking lot into a place of quiet and relaxation. The new square refers to the surrounding neo-Renaissance architecture and unfolds a game of strict geometry, enlivened by differentiated green and the rippling of a fountain.
Placed in the axis of the school building and forming the centre of the courtyard, the fountain consists of a cube of raw steel with vertical slits releasing plenty of water at the centre of a square grid that absorbs the water. The area adjacent to the school building is paved with geometrically rhythmic granite. Opposite is a square lawn bounded by hornbeams, with a limetree in the diagonal. Next to the footpath on the side rises a head-high structure – less fence than endless metal strip that oscillates in passing. The neighbouring building is adjoined by a pergola with climbing roses and benches, complemented by fixed and movable, geometrically rigorous seating in the courtyard. A showpiece of balance, be it of culture and nature or of geometry and coincidence.

Architekt: Architektonická kancelář Burian – Křivinka, Aleš Burian, Gustav Křivinka, Brünn
Bauherr: Region Pardubice
Kategorie: Erschließung und Neubau Öffentlicher Raum
Planung: 2004
Ausführung: 2004–2005
Adresse: Komenského-Platz

Architects: Architektonická kancelář Burian – Křivinka, Aleš Burian, Gustav Křivinka, Brno
Client: Region of Pardubice
Category: Development and new construction, public space
Planning: 2004
Construction: 2004–2005
Address: Komenského Square

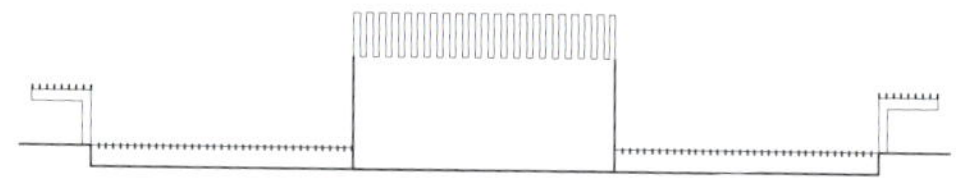

aa

Schnitt Brunnen mit festen Bänken Maßstab 1:50	Section fountain with fixed seating Scale 1:50
Grundriss Maßstab 1:750 1 Brunnen 2 Grünfläche 3 Pergola 4 Zaun 5 Pädagogische Hochschule	Floor plan Scale 1:750 1 Fountain 2 Green space 3 Pergola 4 Fence 5 College of Education

Städtische Akupunktur

Urban Acupuncture

Immer wieder stößt man in der Stadt auf Objekte, die man noch nicht Architektur, doch auch nicht Design nennen würde. Unterhalb des Schlossbergs, an der heiklen Nahtstelle mit der Bürgerstadt, verdichten sie sich – so in der Mariánská-Gasse und deren Verlängerung.
Das beginnt mit der Passage zwischen nördlicher Vorstadt und Zentrum – ein gepflasterter Weg, gefasst von mannshohen Trockenmauern. Städtebau, wie ihn Luigi Snozzi kultiviert hat. Der Weg stößt auf das angehobene Trottoir der Schlossauffahrt und einer Zugangsrampe. Ganz selbstverständlich neigt sich das Plateau, integriert in den Weg, begleitet mit einfachem Geländer. Eine Handreichung, die an Plečnik denken lässt, wenn auch direkter umgesetzt. Weiter abwärts plätschert das Wasser des alten Wäschebrunnens. Ein barocker Wasserspeier, Bossensteine und gesägter Naturstein, ein Holzsteg mit geschmiedetem Geländer fassen die Wasserfläche – Carlo Scarpa lässt grüßen. Einige Häuser weiter blieben zwei Parzellen unbebaut, mit rohem Material gefasst, darin weißer Sand oder Rasen, Baum und Stein – Räume, dem Ungeplanten gewidmet. Am Ende der Gasse ein Haus mit verdrehtem Dach à la John Hejduk für: Wohnen? Arbeiten? Derzeit werden Bilder ausgestellt.

Frequently, you come across objects in the town that you wouldn't call architecture, and neither design. Below the castle hill, at the delicate seam with the civil town, they condense – like in Mariánská Lane and its extension.
It begins with the passage between the northern suburbs and the centre, a paved path framed by head-high drystone walls – urban design as cultivated by Luigi Snozzi. The path meets the raised pavement of the castle entrance and an access ramp. The plateau, integrated with the path, inclines naturally and is accompanied by a simple banister. A "helping hand" that is reminiscent of Plečnik, but implemented more directly. Further down, the water of the old wash fountain gurgles. A baroque gargoyle, ashlar and sawed natural stone, and a wooden walkway with a wrought banister frame the water surface – very much reminiscent of Carlo Scarpa. A few buildings further on, two plots remain undeveloped, framed by raw material, with white sand or lawn, trees and stone inside – spaces dedicated to the unplanned. At the end of the lane, a house with a twisted roof in the style of John Hejduk: For living? For working? Currently, there is an exhibition of paintings here.

Architekt: Zdeňka Vydrová, Brünn; Aleš Burian, Brünn; Josef Pleskot, Prag
Bauherr: Stadt Litomyšl
Kategorie: Erschließung Öffentlicher Raum
Planung: 1997–2008
Ausführung: 1997, 2007, 2014
Adresse: Zahájská, Jiráskova, Mariánská

Architects: Zdeňka Vydrová, Brno; Aleš Burian, Brno; Josef Pleskot, Prague
Client: Municipality of Litomyšl
Category: Development, public space
Planning: 1997–2008
Construction: 1997, 2007, 2014
Address: Zahájská, Jiráskova, Mariánská

Lageplan
Maßstab 1:3000
1. **Passage Zentrum-Vorstadt**
2. **Gehweg mit Rampe**
3. **ehemaliger Wäschebrunnen**
4. **japanischer Garten**
5. **1 ar^{T}-Garten**
6. **Haus im Garten, Galerie**

Site plan
Scale 1:3,000
1. Passage between centre and suburbs
2. Pavement with ramp
3. Former wash fountain
4. Japanese Garden
5. 1 ar^{T} garden
6. House in garden, gallery

Gastlichkeit auf vielen Ebenen

Hospitality on Many Levels

Im eigentlichen Kern der historischen Altstadt, unterhalb des Schlossbergs und des Klostergartens, wurden zwei durch ihre Arkaden herausragende, jahrhundertealte Häuser zum Zentrum eines Hotel- und Gastronomiekomplexes zusammengefasst. Das linke Nachbarhaus wurde abgebrochen und dem historischem Vorbild entsprechend, aber vergrößert wieder aufgebaut. Die ursprünglichen Nebengebäude im rückwärtigen Hof unterhalb des Klostergartens sind neuen Speiseräumen und Freiflächen gewichen.
Die beiden historischen Häuser wurden auf ihre Substanz zurückgeführt, neu verbunden und mit zeitgenössischem Standard für Rezeption, Bar und Gasträume ausgestattet. Der erneuerte Nachbarbau beherbergt nun die gesamte technische Ausstattung sowie die Küche. Die Speiseräume befinden sich in einem Neubau zwischen Hauptgebäude und Klostergarten. Dank seiner transparenten Stahl-Glas-Konstruktion bleibt der introvertierte Charakter des ehemalige Hofs spürbar. Darüber hinaus bleibt Raum für einen intimen Außenbereich. Auf dem Dach des Neubaus erhebt sich, um wenige Sitzbereiche zurückgesetzt, ein gläserner Gästepavillon, von dem aus ein Durchlass in der umschließenden Mauer in den Klostergarten führt. Der Bau vermittelt so zwischen ruhigem Grün und der Umtriebigkeit der städtischen Gasse mit erhöhter Freisitzfläche.

In the very heart of the historic Old Town, below the castle hill and the monastery gardens, two centuries-old buildings characterised by their arcades have been combined to form the centre of a hotel and gastronomical complex. The neighbouring building to the left was demolished and rebuilt as an enlarged version of its historic predecessor. The former outbuildings in the rear courtyard below the monastery gardens have been replaced by new dining halls and open spaces.
The two historical buildings were restored down to their substance, newly connected, and the reception, bar and guest rooms were equipped to meet current standards. The renewed neighbouring building now houses all the technical equipment as well as the kitchen. The dining halls are located in a new building between the main building and the monastery gardens. Thanks to its transparent steel-glass structure, the former courtyard's introverted character remains palpable. In addition, room for an intimate outdoor area has been created. On the roof of the new building rises a glass guest pavilion, set back by a few seating areas, from which a passage in the surrounding wall leads to the monastery gardens. The building's elevated terrace creates a transition between quiet green and the bustle of the urban lane below.

Architekt: Architektonický atelier ABV, Prag
Bauherr: Mega Promotions s.r.o.
Kategorie: Umbau und Sanierung Gastgewerbe
Planung: 1995–2007
Ausführung: 1996–2008
Adresse: Šantovo náměstí 181

Architects: Architektonický atelier ABV, Prague
Client: Mega Promotions s.r.o.
Category: Alteration and renovation, hospitality
Planning: 1995–2007
Construction: 1996–2008
Address: 181 Šantovo Square

RESTAURACE
Bohém
HOTEL
APLAUS

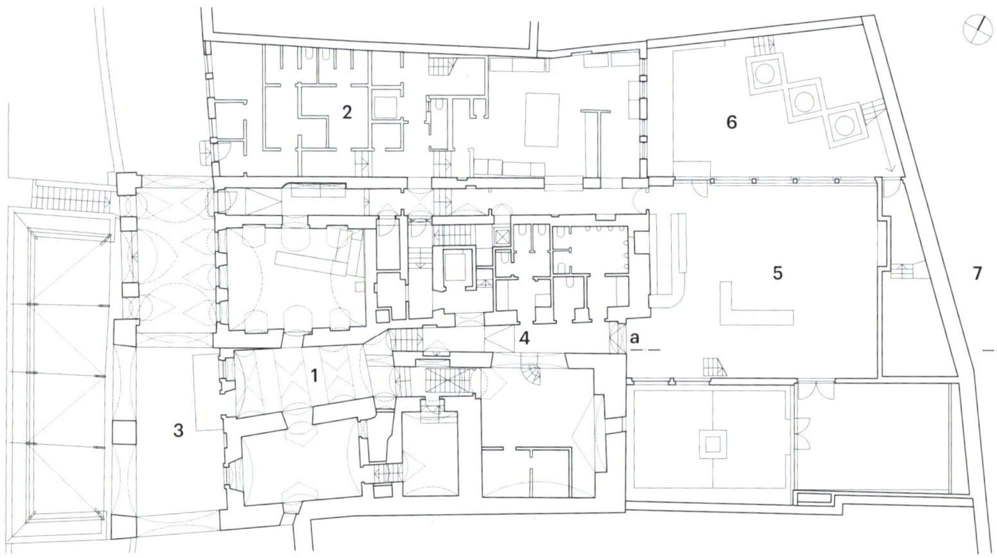
1
2
3
4
5
6
7
a
a

APLAUS HOTEL

Grundriss / Schnitt Restaurant, Dachpavillon
Maßstab 1:400
1 umgebauter Bestand, Rezeption, Bar, Gästezimmer
2 wiederaufgebauter Altbau, Gastronomietechnik
3 Eingang Stadtseite
4 Durchgang Restaurant
5 Restaurant mit Pavillon als Dachaufbau
6 Freisitz im alten Hof
7 Eingang Klostergarten

Floor plan / Section restaurant, roof pavilion
Scale 1:400
1 Converted building, reception, bar, guest rooms
2 Rebuilt old building, catering facilities
3 Entrance from city
4 Passage to restaurant
5 Restaurant with pavilion as roof structure
6 Outdoor seating in the old courtyard
7 Entrance from monastery gardens

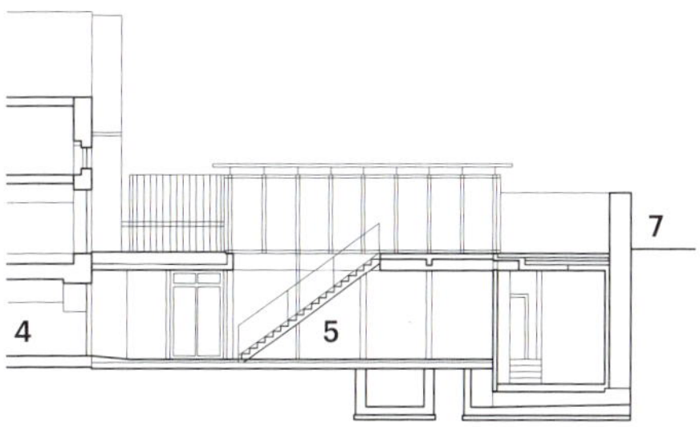

aa

Noblesse in Grau und Weiß

Noblesse in Grey and White

Das zweigeschossige, original erhaltene Bürgerhaus im Empirestil des frühen 19. Jahrhunderts beherbergt heute ein histologisches Labor und eine Dachwohnung. In Abstimmung mit dem Denkmalamt wurde die Straßenfront restauriert; klassische Noblesse in Grau und Weiß blieb verpflichtend. Drei zusätzliche Dachgauben zeigen den Eingriff auf der Straßenseite. Die Gartenseite dagegen wurde durch einen großzügig geöffneten Anbau mit einheitlicher Holzlamellenfassade erweitert. Die Labor- und Büroräume in Erdgeschoss und 1. Stock sind funktional geordnet und betont sachlich; Weiß dominiert, dazu Grautöne, helles Holz und inszeniertes Licht. Eindrucksvoll die zentrale einläufige Treppe mit Podest: eine Komposition aus Glas, Gitterrosten und Kunstlicht. Hier werden zeitgenössische Baustoffe durch virtuose Handhabung nobilitiert.
Ein separates Treppenhaus erschließt die Wohnräume im Dach – eine offene zweigeschossige Raumlandschaft, weiße Flächen, Böden aus Holz. Dachfenster belichten die eine Seite, die sich zur großzügigen Dachterrasse orientiert. Sie bietet einen ganz privaten Freiraum oberhalb der benachbarten Gärten. Introvertiert auch der eigene Gartenhof mit Gräsern und altem Baum, Holzdecks und Sichtmauerwerk, Farn, Kunst und plätscherndem Brunnen.

The originally preserved two-storey townhouse in the early 19th-century Empire style now houses a histological laboratory and a rooftop flat. The street front was restored in consultation with the monuments office, which decided that a classical noble facade in grey and white was obligatory. Only three additional dormers betray the intervention on the street side. The garden side, on the other hand, has received a generously open extension with a uniform wooden lamella facade. The laboratory and office spaces on the ground floor and first floor are functionally arranged and emphatically sober; they are dominated by white colour, with shades of grey, light wood and staged lighting. The central single-flight staircase with a landing is an impressive composition of glass, gratings and artificial light. Contemporary building materials were ennobled by their masterly handling here.
A separate stairwell provides access to the flat in the roof – an open, two-storey spatial landscape with white surfaces and wooden floors. Skylights illuminate the side oriented towards the spacious roof terrace, which provides a very private space above the neighbouring gardens. The flat's own garden courtyard is also rather introverted, with grasses and old trees, wooden decks and exposed masonry, ferns, art and babbling fountains.

Architekt: Molo architekti, Pavel Griz, Karel Šrámek, Patrik Zamazal, Letohrad
Bauherr: Zdeňka Svojanovská
Kategorie: Umbau und Sanierung Wohnhaus, Wohnen und Labor
Planung: 2010
Ausführung: 2011–13
Adresse: Šmilovského 195

Architects: Molo architekti, Pavel Griz, Karel Šrámek, Patrik Zamazal, Letohrad
Client: Zdeňka Svojanovská
Category: Alteration and renovation, residential and laboratory building
Planning: 2010
Construction: 2011–13
Address: Šmilovského 195

Lageplan
Maßstab 1:1000

Grundrisse
Maßstab 1:400
1 Haus mit Labor
2 Garten
3 Smilovského
4 Rektora Striteského
5 Wohnraum, Küche
6 Schlafzimmer, Bad
7 Dachterrasse
8 Zugang und Erschließung Labor
9 Erschließung Dachwohnung
10 Besprechung, Lager, Laborräume

Site plan
Scale 1:1,000

Floor plans
Scale 1:400
1 House with laboratory
2 Garden
3 Smilovského
4 Rektora Striteského
5 Living, kitchen
6 Bedroom, bathroom
7 Roof terrace
8 Laboratory entrance and circulation
9 Access to flat in roof
10 Meetings, storage, lab rooms

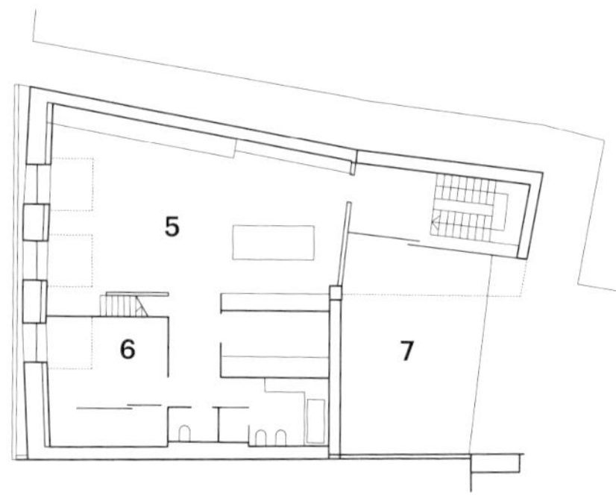

Obergeschoss /
Top floor

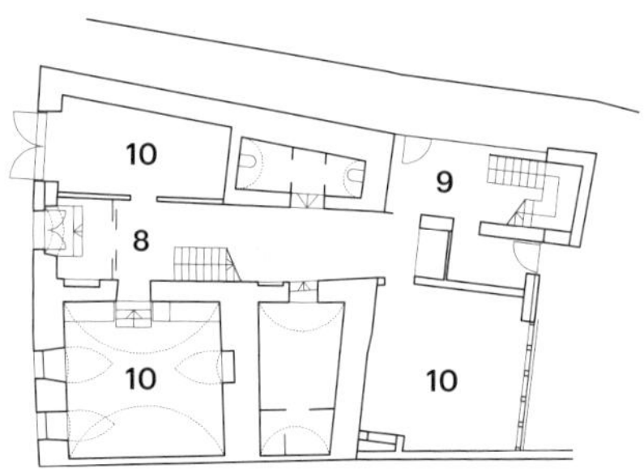

Erdgeschoss /
Ground floor

Ein neues Quartier

A New Neighbourhood

Das große Bauvorhaben der Stadt nach der Wende war die Wohnanlage „beim Krankenhaus". Das aus einem Wettbewerb hervorgegangene städtebauliche Konzept sieht einen nach Süden offenen, aufgelockerten Block mit verkehrsberuhigtem Hofbereich und Zeilen im Inneren vor, der sich flach nach Osten abtreppt. Die meist dreigeschossigen Bauten variieren Zwei- und Dreispänner sowie Laubengangtypen. Bei striktem Verzicht auf historische Reminiszenzen zeigen Gliederung, Maßstäblichkeit, private Vorgärten, Baumaterialien sowie Dachform die neue Bauauffassung.
Die Realisierung geschieht in mehreren Abschnitten, beginnend mit der längsten Zeile des Preisträgerbüros Rudiš Rudiš, das anschließend noch für einen abgewinkelten Kopfbau mit eingefasst überdachter Garage und Spielplatz auf dem Deck verantwortlich zeichnet.
Die nächsten Abschnitte folgen einer Überarbeitung der Planung unter Beibehaltung der Grundfigur. Pleskot fasst die westlichen Einfamilienhäuser zu einer geschlossenen Reihe von Zweispännern mit offenen Stellplätzen zur tieferen Straße zusammen und betont ihre Geschlossenheit und Reihung. Gegenüber liegen senkrecht zwei reine Laubenganghäuser. Deren Vorgartenzone mit kleinen öffentlichen Höfen ist um ein Geschoss zur Straße hin abgesenkt.

The town's big construction project after the Velvet Revolution was the residential complex "at the hospital". The urban design concept, which emerged from a contest, consists of a loosely-laid block open towards the south, with a traffic-calmed courtyard and linear buildings inside, that descends in flat steps towards to the east. The mostly three-storey buildings vary between two or three flats per storey grouped around staircases and arcade types. Strictly renouncing historical reminiscences, the organisation, scale, private front gardens, building materials and roof shapes demonstrate a new approach to building.
Construction took place in several sections, starting with the longest linear building by the award-winning Rudiš Rudiš office, which was also responsible for an angled building at the end that encloses a covered garage and a playground on the deck.
The next sections followed a revised plan, while maintaining the basic figure. Pleskot combined the western single-family houses into a continuous row of buildings with two flats per storey grouped around staircases and open parking spaces towards the lower street, emphasising their unity and sequence. Opposite are two perpendicular arcade buildings. Their front garden area with small public courtyards is lowered towards the street by one storey.

Architekt: Viktor Rudiš, Martin Rudiš, Brünn
Josef Pleskot / AP atelier, Prag
Bauherr: Stadt Litomyšl
Kategorie: Neubau und Geschosswohnbau
Planung: 1994 – 2003 A1, A4, A2, A3, A5
Ausführung: 1997–2005
Adresse: Z. kopala, Jana Evangelisty Purkyně

Architects: Viktor Rudiš, Martin Rudiš, Brno
Josef Pleskot / AP atelier, Prague
Client: Municipality of Litomyšl
Category: New buildings, multistorey residential buildings
Planning: 1994 – 2003 A1, A4, A2, A3, A5
Construction: 1997–2005
Address: Z. kopala, Jana Evangelisty Purkyně

Lageplan
Maßstab 1:2000

1. **Erster Bauabschnitt, Rudiš/Rudiš, Zweispänner**
2. **Zweiter Bauabschnitt, Pleskot, Laubengang**
3. **Dritter Bauabschnitt, Rudiš/Rudiš, Zweispänner, Kinderspielplatz auf Tiefgarage**
4. **Vierter Bauabschnitt, Pleskot, Zweispänner auf Garagen**
5. **Haupterschließung Z. Kopala**

Site plan
Scale 1:2,000

1. First section, Rudiš/Rudiš, two flats per floor
2. Second section, Pleskot, arcade
3. Third section, Rudiš/Rudiš, two flats per floor, playground on covered garage
4. Fourth section, Pleskot, two flats per floor above garages
5. Main circulation, Z. Kopala

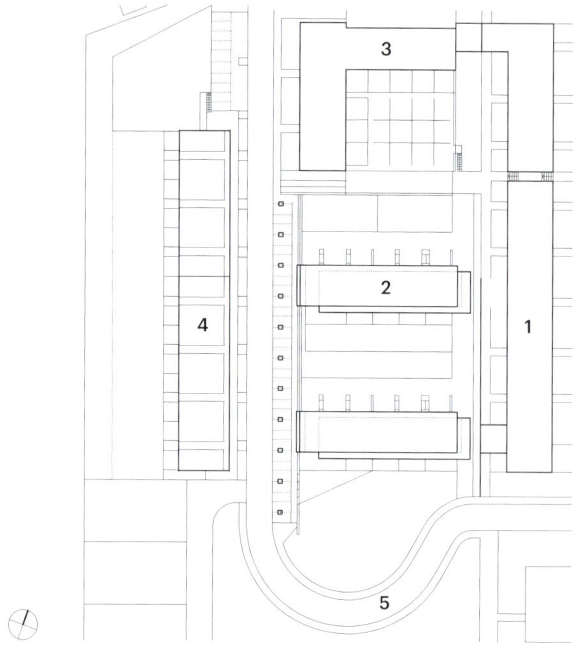

Den Jungen ein Zuhause

A Home for the Young

Das Studentenwohnheim ergänzt ein 25 Jahre älteres Wohnheim um zwei neue Trakte, die zusammen einen Hof einschließen. Nun bieten sie Unterkunft für 120 Studenten der pädagogischen Hochschule, in den Ferien auch für Teilnehmer der Sportwettkämpfe der nahen Sportanlage.
Die Architekten legten Wert darauf, den Bewohnern ein wirkliches Zuhause zu bieten. Dies gelingt durch Gliederung und Übersichtlichkeit sowie bescheidenen Luxus der Anlage. Konstruktion und Proportion der stereometrischen Volumen verleihen ihr einen noblen Anstrich. Dazu tragen die französischen Fenster mit hölzernen Schiebeläden bei. Die Zweibettzimmer sind entlang eines Korridors gereiht, ihre Balkone orientieren sich Richtung Landschaft oder Stadt. Zur Straße hin ist eine Seite des Korridors aufgeglast, wodurch der belebte Eindruck des Hauses bestärkt wird. Eine ebenfalls verglaste Brücke bindet den Altbau an. Im Erdgeschoss des Mittelbaus liegt zum Hof ein natürlich belichteter Speisesaal, zur Straße hin sind Nebenräume und Küche ausgerichtet. Der Hof steht mit Grillplatz und Sportflächen der Erholung aller Bewohner zur Verfügung.

The student residence adds two new wings to a 25 years older residence, which together enclose a courtyard. The buildings provide accommodation for 120 students of the College of Education and, during the holidays, also for participants of the sports competitions at the nearby sports complex.
The architects attached great importance to providing the residents with a real home. They succeeded thanks to the structure and clarity as well as modest luxury of their design. Construction and proportion of the stereometric volumes give them a classy feel, for example in form of the French windows with wooden sliding shutters. The twin rooms are arranged along a corridor, their balconies are oriented towards the landscape or the town. The side of the corridor facing the street is glazed, which reinforces the lively impression the house makes. A likewise glazed bridge connects to the old building. On the ground floor of the central building, towards the courtyard, is a naturally lit dining hall, while ancillary rooms and the kitchen are arranged on the street side. The courtyard's barbecue area and sports areas offer relaxation for the residents.

Architekt: Architektonická kancelář Burian – Křivinka, Aleš Burian, Gustav Křivinka, Brünn
Bauherr: Stadt Litomyšl
Kategorie: Neubau Wohnbau
Planung: 2001
Ausführung: 2002–2003
Adresse: Strakovská 1071

Architects: Architektonická kancelář Burian – Křivinka, Aleš Burian, Gustav Křivinka, Brno
Client: Municipality of Litomyšl
Category: New building, residential building
Planning: 2001
Construction: 2002–2003
Address: Strakovská 1071

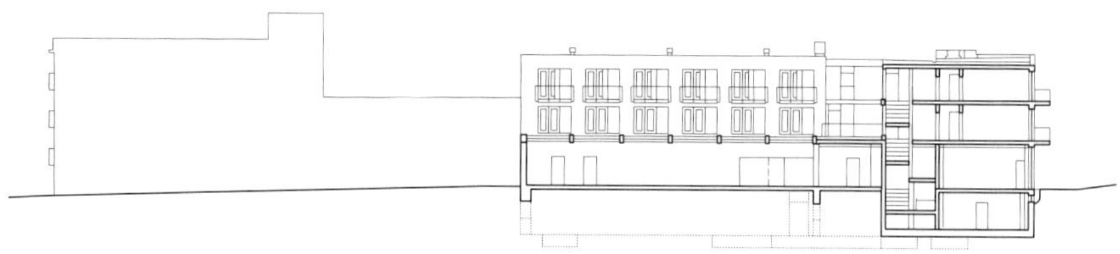

aa

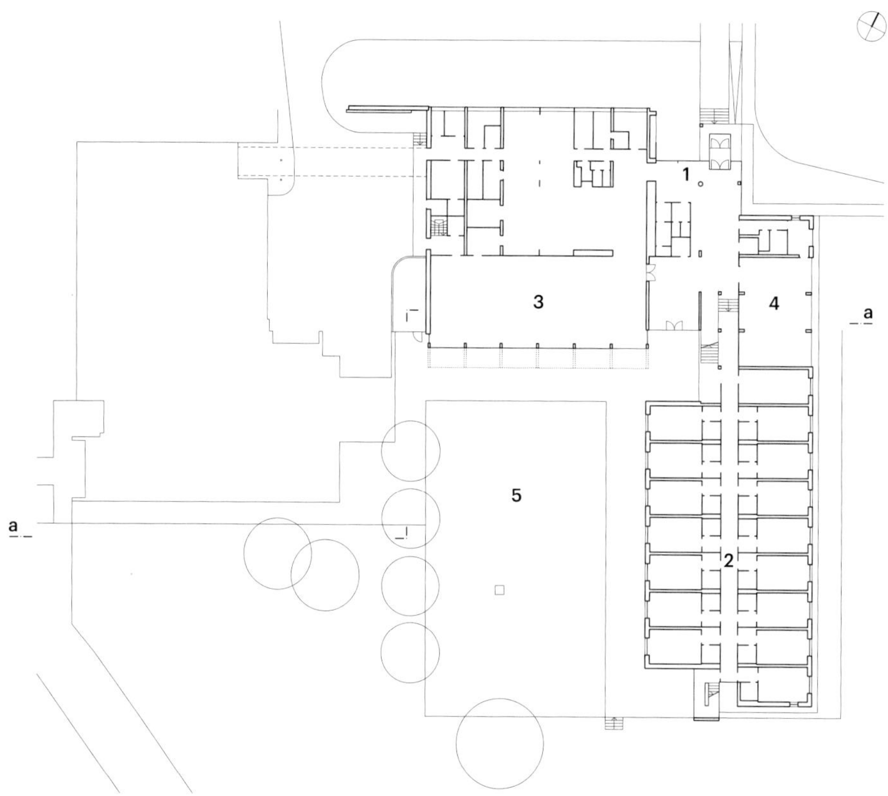

Schnitt / Grundriss
Maßstab 1:750
1 Empfang
2 Studentenapartments
3 Mensa
4 Auditorium
5 Freizeithof

Section / Floor plan
Scale 1:750
1 Reception
2 Student flats
3 Mensa
4 Auditorium
5 Courtyard for leisure activities

Der Charme des knappen Budgets

The Charm of the Tight Budget

Zu den Sportanlagen südöstlich der Altstadt gehören auch Tennisplätze. Das Areal wurde Ende der 1990er-Jahre um eine Tennishalle mit Squashräumen, Sportgaststätte und Platzwartwohnung ergänzt. Die Halle nimmt drei Fünftel des kompakten Volumens ein, den dreigeschossigen Rest teilen sich Umkleiden, Squashräume, davor das Restaurant, darüber die Wohnung.
Herausforderung war ein knappes Budget; gemeistert wurde es durch Einsatz industrieller Halbzeuge. Die Stahlkonstruktion ist eine Standardhalle, die Außenhaut aus zementgebundenen Platten, das flachgeneigte Dach aus ebensolcher Welle. Die liegend verbauten Platten ergeben eine horizontale Bänderung, die nach Bedarf differenziert Fenster integriert. Innen dominieren großflächig OSB-Spanplatten, Sichtbeton und Farbe. Die „armen" Materialien werden nobilitiert durch wohlüberlegte Verarbeitung, ob in Proportion oder Detail. Die Halle: blauer Sportboden, roher Holzwerkstoff, roter Stahl, ein Fensterband. Das Restaurant: ruppiger Charme bei der Einrichtung mit der Möglichkeit, es mittels Schiebetor im Sommer zur Loggia zu öffnen. Die Gänge: künstlerisch belebt durch abstrakte Muster in kräftig bunten Farben. Ein überzeugendes Beispiel für Gestaltungsqualität ohne großes Budget.

The sports facilities south-east of the Old Town also include tennis courts. The site was supplemented in the late 1990s by a tennis hall with squash courts, a sports restaurant and a flat for the groundskeeper. The hall occupies three-fifths of the compact volume, the three-storey rest is shared by changing rooms and squash courts, the restaurant in front of them and the flat above. The tight budget presented a challenge, which was mastered by using semi-finished industrial products. The steel structure is a standard hall, the outer skin made of cement-bonded slabs, the flat-sloping roof of corrugated sheets. The horizontally installed panels result in a horizontal banding that is able to integrate windows as needed. The interior is dominated by OSB particle board, exposed concrete and paint. The "poor" materials were ennobled by carefully considered processing, whether in proportion or detail. The hall: a blue sports floor, raw wood material, red steel, a ribbon of windows. The restaurant: gruff charm in the interior, with the possibility of opening a sliding gate towards the loggia in the summer. The corridors: artistically animated by abstract patterns in bright colours. A compelling example of design quality without a big budget.

Architekt: Petr Hrůša, Petr Pelčák, Brünn
Bauherr: Stadt Litomyšl
Kategorie: Neubau Sport- und Freizeitanlagen
Planung: 1997–1998
Ausführung: 1998–1999
Adresse: U Plovárny

Architects: Petr Hrůša, Petr Pelčák, Brno
Client: Municipality of Litomyšl
Category: New building, sports and leisure facilities
Planning: 1997–1998
Construction: 1998–1999
Address: U Plovárny

Grundriss
Maßstab 1:750
1 Zugang
2 Tennishalle
3 Kegelbahn
4 Squashfelder
5 Bar, Restaurant
6 Freischankfläche

Floor plan
Scale 1:750
1 Entrance
2 Tennis hall
3 Bowling alley
4 Squash courts
5 Bar, restaurant
6 Outside bar

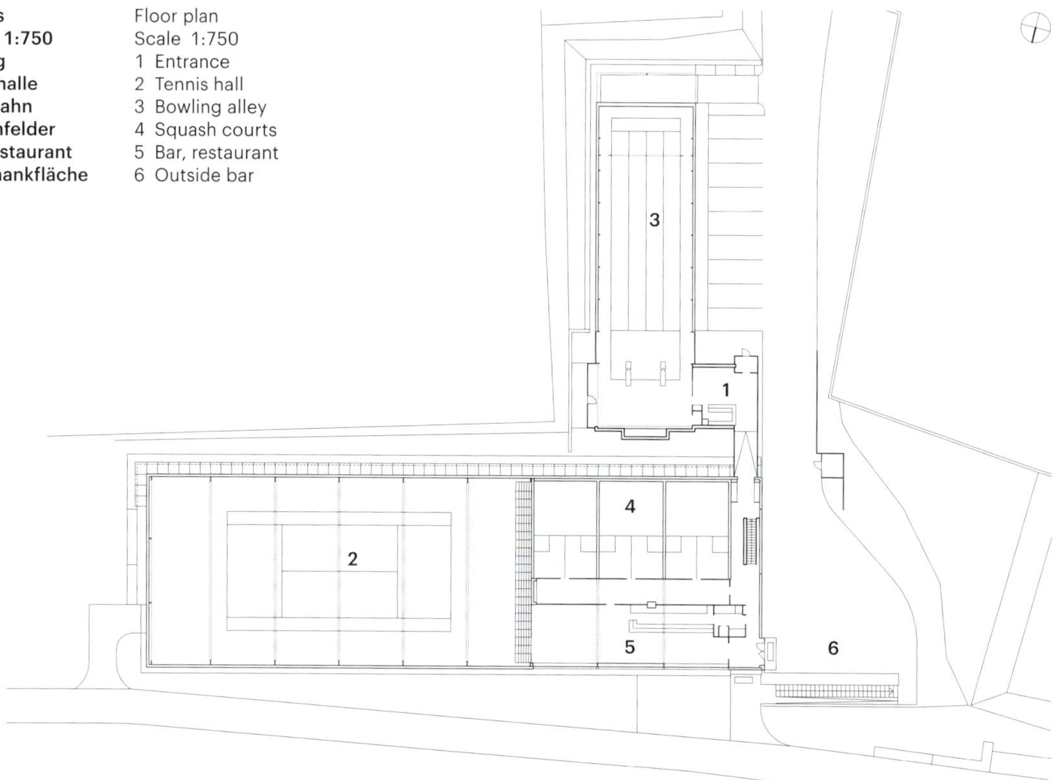

Heitere Spiele

Cheerful Games

Nahe der Altstadt liegen Sportanlagen, die Zug um Zug saniert und erneuert wurden. 2003 erhielt die offene Arena einen gedeckten Tribünenbau. An der westlichen Längsseite des Platzes bieten, aufsitzend auf die Räume des Sportclubs, des Kiosks, der Umkleiden, WC-Anlagen und Technik, ansteigende Stuhlreihen Sitzplätze für 530 Besucher. Erdgeschossig wird die Ansicht der Betonkonstruktion durch Lärchenwände überspielt, darüber durch farbige Sitzschalen in rot, gelb und grün. Ein Dutzend zeltförmige Membranen aus PVC-verstärktem Polyestergewebe bilden den schwebenden Dachabschluss, aufgespannt in eine galvanisierte Stahlrohrkonstruktion. Sie strahlen ein heitere Leichtigkeit aus, wie sie bei neuen Sportanlagen Englands zu finden ist.
Drei Jahre später wurde die Eislauffläche eingehaust. Die Längsseiten mit den Tribünen sind gegliedert durch acht monumentale Betonstützen, steil aufstrebend und V-förmig gespreizt, darauf ruhen räumliche Fachwerkträger, deren Untergurte die Holzkonstruktion des Dachs tragen. Dazwischen gespannt das Holzgefach der Wände, innen mit Zementfaserplatten, außen mit Polycarbonat verkleidet. Die Belichtung über Dachträger, unter dem Vordach und neben den Stützen betont die Konstruktion. 2007 war die Eislaufhalle für den Mies van der Rohe Award nominiert.

Near the Old Town are sports facilities that were renovated and renewed step by step. In 2003, the open arena received a covered grandstand. On the western long side of the arena, sitting on top of the rooms of the sports clubs, the kiosk, the dressing rooms, WC facilities and technology, ascending rows of seats provide seating for 530 spectators. The concrete structure is concealed by larch walls on the ground floor, and by coloured seats in red, yellow and green above. A dozen tent-shaped membranes made of PVC-reinforced polyester fabric form the floating roof, mounted in a galvanised steel tube construction. They radiate a cheerful lightness as found in contemporary sports facilities in England.
Three years later, the ice rink was enclosed. The long sides with the grandstands are divided by eight monumental concrete columns, steeply rising and spread in a V-shape, on which rest spatial lattice girders whose lower chords bear the roof's wooden structure. In between is the wooden framing of the walls, covered with cement fiber panels on the inside and with polycarbonate on the outside. Lighting above roof beams, under the canopy and next to the columns emphasises the construction. In 2007, the skating hall was nominated for the Mies van der Rohe Award.

Architekt: Architektonická kancelář Burian – Křivinka, Ales Burian, Gustav Křivinka, Brünn
Bauherr: Stadt Litomyšl
Kategorie: Neubau Sport- und Freizeit
Planung: 2001, 2002
Ausführung: 2002–2003, 2002–2006
Adresse: U Plovárny

Architects: Architektonická kancelář Burian – Křivinka, Ales Burian, Gustav Křivinka, Brno
Client: Municipality of Litomyšl
Category: New building, sports and leisure facility
Planning: 2001, 2002
Construction: 2002–2003, 2002–2006
Address: U Plovárny

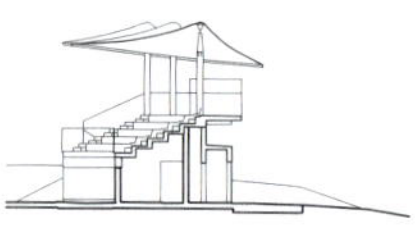

Schnitt Tribüne /
Section grandstand

Schnitte
Maßstab 1:750
1. **Fachwerkträger auf V-förmigen Betonstützen**
2. **Nachträglich aufgehängte Hülle aus Polycarbonplatten, zementgebundene Holzfaserplatten und Holzriegel**

Sections
Scale 1:750
1. Lattice girders on V-shaped concrete columns
2. Retrofitted suspended envelope of polycarbonate panels, cement fibre panels and wooden beams

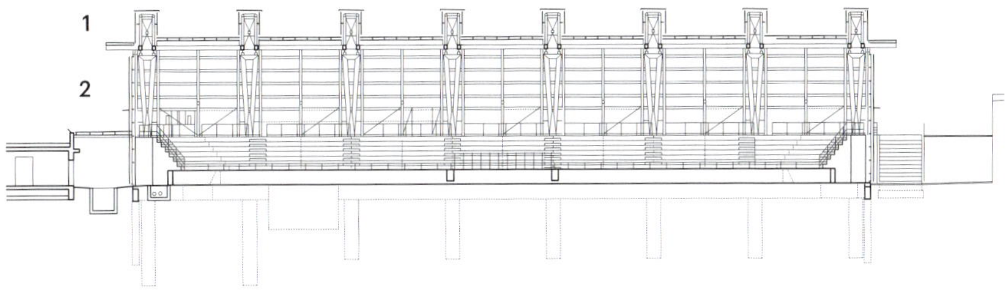

Längsschnitt Überdachung und Einhausung Eisstadion

Longitudinal section roof and envelope of ice rink

Vom Wasser lernen

Learning from the Water

Das neue Hallenbad mit zwei Innenbecken, Whirlpool, Außenbecken, kleiner Bar und Nebenräumen ist ganz aus der Landschaft entwickelt. Aus der Wiese steigen neun gegeneinander versetzte Dachbahnen auf, die mit ihrer Anspielung auf Wellen das Thema ankündigen: eine zweigeschossige Halle, den Freuden des Wassers gewidmet, mit flach geneigtem Dach und zweiseitig unbegrenztem Blick ins Grüne und aufs angrenzende Freibad.
Die Anlage ist streng orthogonal organisiert und gleicht im Schnitt einer Halle mit flach geneigtem Satteldach. Unterm First die durchgehende Trennwand zwischen Halle und dienenden Räumen. Ihre räumliche Durchbildung lässt sie leicht, bewegt und licht wirken.
Atmosphärisch spielen das Blau der Wasserflächen, das Weiß der Wände und Decke, deren sichtbare Leimholzbinder den Rhythmus der „Wellen" aufnimmt, das Anthrazit des Bodens und die Präsenz der parkartigen Umgebung zusammen. Eine vorgelagerte Wasserrutsche mit Treppenturm unterstreicht das Spielerische. Landschaftsbezug und ungewöhnliche Details, etwa der Übergang vom Dach zur Glasfassade, brachten dem Bau als herausragendes Beispiel organisch-expressiver Architektur 2011 den Großen Preis der Tschechischen Architekten-Gesellschaft ein.

The new aquatic centre with two indoor pools, a whirlpool, an outdoor pool, a small bar and ancillary rooms was very much developed from the landscape. From the meadow rise nine roofing sheets offset from each other, which herald the theme by hinting at waves: a two-storey hall, dedicated to the joys of water, with a flat roof and unlimited views of the landscape and the adjacent outdoor pool on two sides.
The complex is organised in a strictly orthogonal manner, similar in section to a hall with a flat pitched roof. Under the ridge, the continuous dividing wall between the hall and ancillary rooms. Its spatial formation makes it feel light, full of movement and bright.
In terms of atmosphere, the blue of the water surfaces, the whiteness of the walls and ceiling, whose exposed glued laminated wood beams take up the rhythm of the "waves", the anthracite of the floor and the presence of the park-like surroundings all form a whole. A waterslide in front, with a stair tower, underlines the playful approach. Its rooting in the landscape and unusual details, such as the transition from the roof to the glass facade, earned the building the Grand Prize of the Czech Architects Society in 2011, as an outstanding example of organic-expressive architecture.

Architekt: DRNH architektonická kancelár, Antonín Novák, Petr Valenta, Radovan Smejkal, Radek Štefka, Brünn
Bauherr: Stadt Litomyšl
Kategorie: Neubau Freizeitanlage
Planung: 2006
Ausführung: 2009–2010
Adresse: U Plovárny 1221

Architects: DRNH architektonická kancelár, Antonín Novák, Petr Valenta, Radovan Smejkal, Radek Štefka, Brno
Client: Municipality of Litomyšl
Category: New building, leisure facility
Planning: 2006
Construction: 2009–2010
Address: U Plovárny 1221

Lageplan
Maßstab 1:1500
Schnitt / Grundriss
Maßstab 1:750
1 neues Hallenbad
2 Freibad 1938 und folgend
3 überdachte Tribühne
4 Eissporthalle
5 Schwimmhalle
6 Umkleiden
7 Bar neben Eingang
8 Turm mit Wasser-rutsche
9 Außenbecken

Site plan
Scale 1:1,500
Section / Floor plan
Scale 1:750
1 New indoor pool
2 Outdoor pool since 1938
3 Covered stand
4 Ice skating facility
5 Indoor pool
6 Changing rooms
7 Bar beside entrance
8 Tower with water slide
9 Outdoor pool

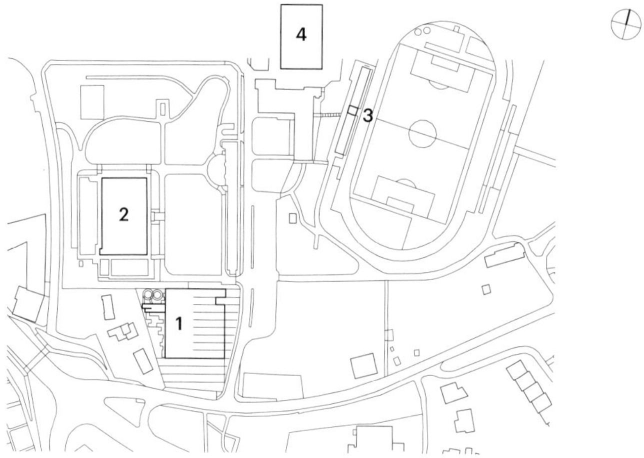

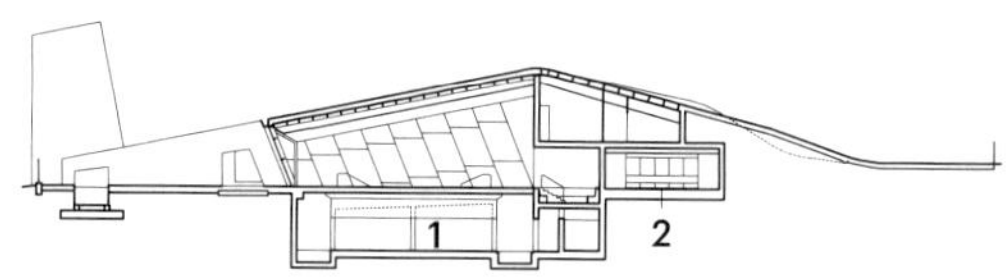

aa

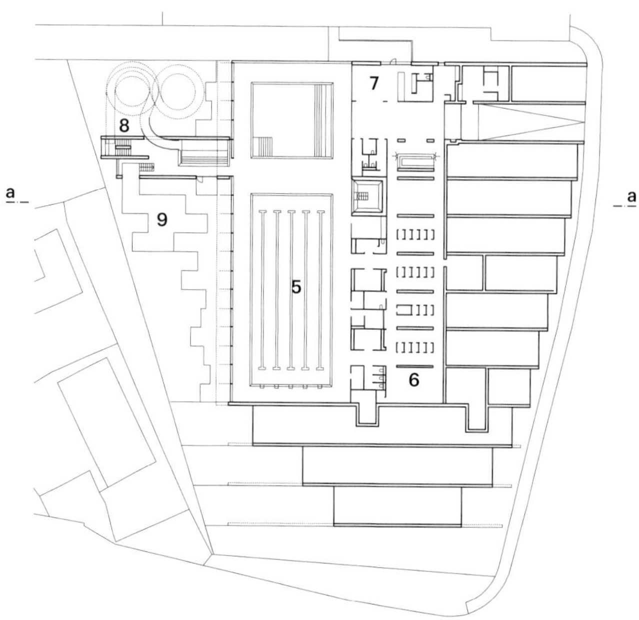

Arkaden der Vorstadt

Arcades of the Suburbs

Mit dem Bau der Durchgangsstraße Anfang der 1980er-Jahre verfiel das Belidla-Viertel südlich der Altstadt. Ein überdimensionierter Busbahnhof brachte keine Verbesserung. 2000 beschloss die Stadt eine Neuordnung.
Das traf sich mit dem Interesse eines internationalen Lebensmittelkonzerns an diesem zentralen Standort. Die Stadt nahm Verhandlungen auf unter der Bedingung, dass der Supermarktbetreiber im Rahmen eines Gesamtkonzepts einen neuen verkleinerten Busbahnhof in anspruchsvoller Architektur finanzierte. Eine internationale Exkursion war Teil der intensiven Beratung des Gemeinderats, der sich schließlich durchsetzte.
Das innovative städtebauliche Konzept: zwei Bauten mit verwandtem Auftritt und anspruchsvoller Mitte. Das Klinkerkleid von Supermarkt und Wartegebäude für den Busbahnhof betont die Volumen mit flachem Dach. Zur Mitte schaffen vorgelagerte Arkaden in Holzbauweise einen würdigen Maßstab. Vor dem Wartegebäude reihen sich die Busse auf. Im Schnittfeld beider Bauten entwickelt sich ein artifizieller Gräser- und Blumengarten. Seitlich, neben dem Supermarkt, liegen dessen Parkplätze – an der Peripherie, überdacht durch eine halbkreisförmige Allee. Kleine Läden an der Rückseite der Wartehalte vermitteln zum angrenzenden Wohngebiet.

With the construction of the through-road in the early 1980s, the Belidla neighbourhood south of the Old Town went into decay. An oversized bus station brought no improvement. In 2000, the municipality decided to reorganise the area.
Coincidentally, an international food company was also interested in this central site. The municipality entered into negotiations on condition that the supermarket operator fund a new, scaled-down bus station with sophisticated architecture, as part of an overall concept. The town council even went on an international excursion during its consultation process, and finally prevailed.
The innovative urban planning concept consists of two buildings with a similar appearance and a sophisticated centre. The clinker facade of the supermarket and the waiting hall for the bus station emphasises the flat-roofed volumes. Towards the centre, wooden arcades create an appropriate scale in front. The buses line up outside the waiting hall. In the intersection of both buildings, an artificial grass and flower garden is being developed. On the site's periphery, in a semicircular avenue, are the supermarket's parking spaces. Small shops at the back of the waiting hall create a smooth transition towards the adjacent residential area.

Architekt: Zdeňka Vydrová, Zdeněk Sendler (Städtebau, Grün), Brünn;
Atelier RAW, Tomáš Rusín, Ivan Wahla, Lukáš Vágner, Brünn
Bauherr: Billa, Stadt Litomyšl
Kategorie: Neubau und Verkehrs- und Geschäftsbau
Planung: 2005–2006
Ausführung: 2006–2008
Adresse: Tomáše G. Masaryka / Mařákova

Architects: Zdeňka Vydrová, Zdeněk Sendler (urban design, green areas), Brno;
Atelier RAW, Tomáš Rusín, Ivan Wahla, Lukáš Vágner, Brno
Client: Billa, Municipality of Litomyšl
Category: New building, traffic and commercial building
Planning: 2005–2006
Construction: 2006–2008
Address: Tomáše G. Masaryka / Mařákova

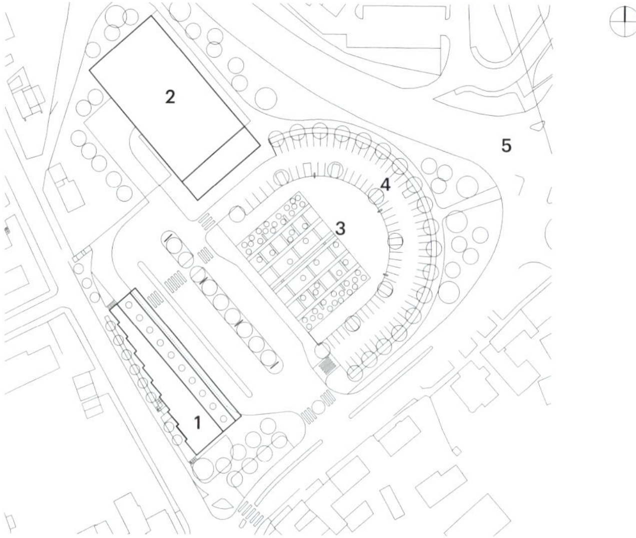
1
2
3
4
5

Lageplan
Maßstab 1:2000
Schnitt Busbahnhof
Maßstab 1:400
1 Busbahnhof mit Warteräumen und rückwärtig Läden
2 Supermarkt
3 Kräuter- und Blumenpark
4 Parkplätze
5 Hauptortsdurchfahrt

Site plan
Scale 1:2000
Section bus station
Scale 1:400
1 Bus station with waiting rooms and shops on the rear
2 Supermarket
3 Herb and flower park
4 Parking
5 Main through-road

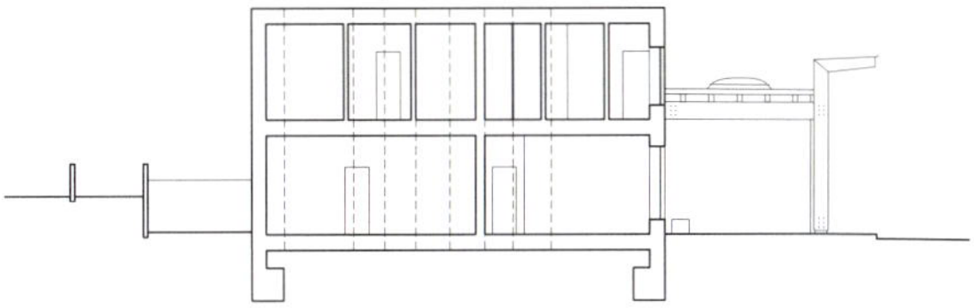

Empor zum Kreuz aus Glas

Upwards to the Cross of Glass

Die 1910 hier gegründete Bruderschafts-Kongregation Litomyšl, den Mährischen Brüdern verpflichtet, bezieht erstmals ein eigenes Gottes- und Gemeindehaus. Den Grund stellte die Gemeinde Litomyšl unter Bürgermeister Kortyš mit der Verpflichtung zu exzellenter Architektur. Motto des Gebäudes: „Deine Güte reicht soweit der Himmel ist, deine Wahrheit soweit die Wolken gehen." Himmelwärts geht die aufsteigende Geste des aus dem Terrain ansteigenden, gefalteten Dachs, gipfelnd im gläsernen Kreuz nach einem Entwurf von Václav Cigler. Die Räume tauchen ins geneigte Terrain, dem Lärm der nahen Straße entzogen. Sichtbeton und Mattglas prägen den Neubau, betonen seine minimalistisch-skulpturale Prägnanz. Voller Lichtsymbolik ist das Kreuz aus dem entstofflichsten aller Stoffe, dem Glas.
Der Zugang erfolgt hangabseitig. Ein breiter Mittelkorridor empfängt die Gemeinde. Der Kirchenraum links mit ansteigender Lichtdecke und Mattglas-Oberlicht ist in Licht und Weiß getaucht. Kunst unterstreicht die sakrale Atmosphäre. Gegenüber liegt der zweigeschossige Trakt mit Gemeinderäumen und Priesterwohnung. Kirchen- und Stadtgemeinde teilen sich zu verschiedenen Anlässen den Kirchenraum. Die Nominierung für den Mies van der Rohe-Award 2012 belegt die internationale Anerkennung als herausragenden Kirchenbau.

The Brotherhood Congregation of Litomyšl, founded here in 1910 and committed to the Moravian Brethren, now has its own church and parish hall for the first time. The plot was provided by the municipality under mayor Kortyš on the condition of an excellent design.
The building's motto: "Your love, Lord, reaches to the heavens, your faithfulness to the skies." The folded roof rises from the terrain towards the sky in an ascending gesture, culminating in a glass cross designed by Václav Cigler. The rooms dip into the sloping terrain, withdrawn from the noise of the nearby street. The new building is characterised by exposed concrete and frosted glass, which accentuate its minimalist, sculptural distinctiveness. As a symbol of light, the cross is made of the most devoid of all substances: glass.
The building is accessed on the slope side. A broad central corridor welcomes the congregation. The church space on the left, with a rising luminous ceiling and frosted-glass skylight, is bathed in light and white colour. Artwork underscores the sacred atmosphere. Opposite is the two-storey wing with community rooms and the vicar's residence. The church and the municipality share the church space for different events. Its nomination for the 2012 Mies van der Rohe Award attests to international recognition as an outstanding church building.

Architekt: Zdeněk Fránek, Brünn
Bauherr: Církev bratrská Litomyšl
Kategorie: Neubau Sakralbau
Planung: 2007
Ausführung: 2008–2010
Adresse: Moravská 1222

Architects: Zdeněk Fránek, Brno
Client: Církev bratrská Litomyšl
Category: New building, sacred building
Planning: 2007
Construction: 2008–2010
Address: Moravská 1222

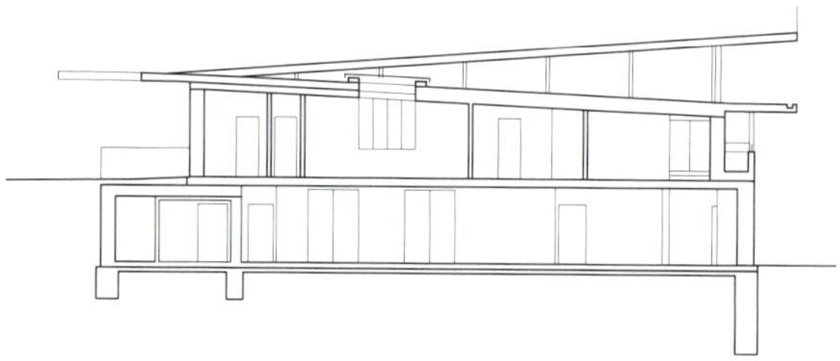

aa

Schnitt / Grundrisse
Maßstab 1:400
1 Zugang und Foyer
2 Kirchenraum
3 Gemeinderäume, Nebenräume
4 Pfarrwohnung
5 Luftraum Kirche
6 Dach

Section / Floor plans
Scale 1:400
1 Entrance and foyer
2 Church interior
3 Congregational rooms, ancillary rooms
4 Parsonage
5 Airspace church
6 Roof

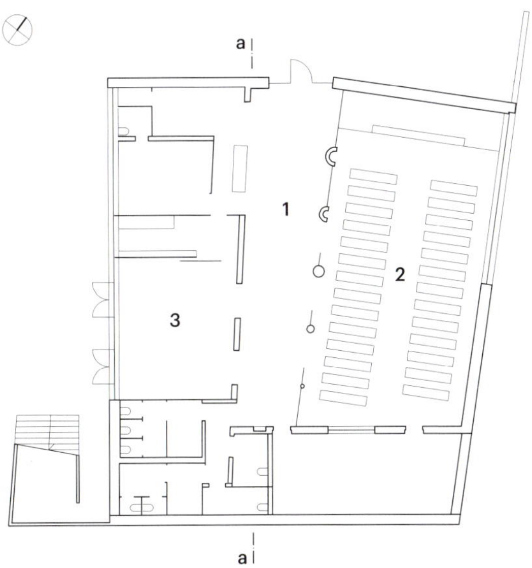

Erdgeschoss /
Ground floor

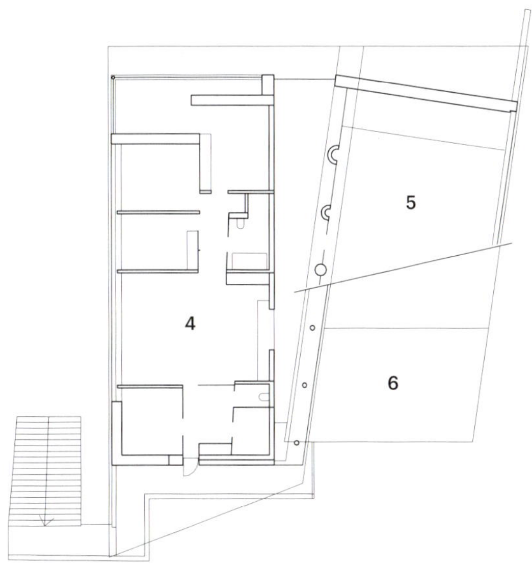

Obergeschoss /
Upper floor

FLORIAN AICHER

Geboren 1954 in Ulm, wo er auf dem Campus der Hochschule für Gestaltung Ulm aufwuchs. Nach dem Architekturstudium an der Staatsbauschule Stuttgart arbeitete er als Architekt bei Werner Wirsing in München und machte sich dort 1981 selbstständig. Aicher unterrichtete an Hochschulen in Deutschland und Österreich, zuletzt an der Fachhochschule Kärnten. Er veröffentlichte zahlreiche Bücher und Beiträge in internationalen Zeitschriften zu Fragen des Bauens und zum Handwerk. Ausgehend von der Entwicklung des Bauens in Vorarlberg gilt sein Interesse den kulturellen Bedingungen, unter denen Architektur sich entfaltet. Seit 2005 lebt Florian Aicher in Rotis im Allgäu.

TOMÁŠ VALENA

Geboren 1950 in Prag, emigrierte 1965 nach Deutschland. Er studierte Philosophie, Kunstgeschichte und Architektur, zunächst in Ljubljana, dann an der Technischen Universität München, später an der Cornell University (USA). Ab 1987 war er als freier Architekt in München tätig und außerdem mit Forschung und umfangreicher Lehrtätigkeit beschäftigt, unter anderem in Ithaca (USA), Ljubljana, München. Valena ist Autor der Standardwerke „Stadt und Topographie“ und „Beziehungen, über den Ortsbezug in der Architektur“. Von 1994 bis 2015 war er Professor für Städtebau und Entwerfen an der Architekturfakultät der Hochschule München. 2019 ist er in München verstorben.

FLORIAN AICHER

Born in Ulm in 1954, where he grew up on the campus of the Ulm School of Design. After studying architecture at the Staatsbauschule Stuttgart, he worked as an architect with Werner Wirsing in Munich and started his own studio in 1981. Aicher taught at universities in Germany and Austria, most recently at the Carinthia University of Applied Sciences. He has published numerous books and articles in international journals on construction and crafts. Based on the development of building in Vorarlberg, his interest is in the cultural conditions under which architecture evolves. Florian Aicher has been living in Rotis in the Allgäu region since 2005.

TOMÁŠ VALENA

Born in Prague in 1950, emigrated to Germany in 1965. He studied philosophy, art history and architecture, first in Ljubljana, then at the Technical University of Munich, later at Cornell University (US). From 1987, he worked as a freelance architect in Munich and also engaged in research and extensive teaching activity, including in Ithaca (US), Ljubljana, and Munich. Valena is the author of the standard works “Stadt und Topographie” (“City and Topography”), “Beziehungen, über den Ortsbezug in der Architektur” (“Relationships, on Location in Architecture”). From 1994 to 2015 he was Professor for Urban Development and Building at the Department of Architecture of the University of Applied Sciences Munich. He died in Munich in 2019.

Architektonický atelier ABV
Pod Starkou 4
CZ-14000 Praha 4
abv.cz

Eva Antošová
Dětská 2442/43
CZ-10000 Praha 10

Václav Babka
Dunajská 29
CZ-625 00 Brno
v.babka@gmail.com

Architektonická kancelář Burian – Křivinka
Aleš Burian, Gustav Křivinka
Kalvodova 13
CZ-60200 Brno
burian-krivinka.cz

Fránek Architects
Zdeněk Fránek
Kamenná 835/13
CZ-63900 Brno
franekarchitects.cz

Molo architekti
Pavel Griz, Karel Šrámek, Patrik Zamazal
Přístavní 1363/1
CZ-17000 Praha 7
moloarchitekti.cz

HŠH architekti
Petr Hájek, Tomáš Hradečný, Jan Šépka
Grafická 831/20
CZ-15000 Praha 5
hsharchitekti.cz

Architekti Hrůša & spol., Ateliér Brno, s.r.o.
Petr Hrůša
Žižkova 5
CZ-60200 Brno
hrusa-atelierbrno.cz

Hulec & Špička architekti
Mikuláš Hulec
Na Bitevní pláni 1180/44
CZ-14000 Praha 4
hs-architekti.cz

Radko Květ
Opletalova 600/6
CZ-60200 Brno-střed
kvetarch.cz

DRNH architektonická kancelář
Antonín Novák, Petr Valenta
Průchodní 2
CZ-60200 Brno
drnh.cz

Pelčák a partner architekti
Petr Pelčák
Dominikánské náměstí 656/2
CZ-60200 Brno
pelcak.cz

AP atelier
Josef Pleskot
Komunardů 1529/5
CZ-17000 Praha 7
apatelier.cz

Rudiš – Rudiš architekti s.r.o
Viktor Rudiš, Martin Rudiš
Jaselská 21
CZ-60200 Brno
rudis-rudis.cz

Atelier RAW s.r.o.
Tomáš Rusín, Ivan Wahla, Lukáš Vágner
Domažlická 12
CZ-61200 Brno
raw.cz

Rusina Frei architekti
Martin Rusina, Martin Frei
Bubenská 225/49
CZ-17000 Praha 7
rusinafrei.cz

Zdeněk Sendler
Česká 6
CZ-60200 Brno
arch.cz/sendler

Atelier Štěpán
Marek Štěpán, Vanda Štěpánova
Kremličkova 6a
CZ-62100 Brno-Řečkovice
atelier-stepan.cz

Zdeňka Vydrová
Jaselská 21
CZ-602 00 Brno

DANK

Den Hinweis auf Litomyšl verdanke ich Matthias Mulitzer, Architekt. Der Gemeinde und ihren Bürgermeistern, unersetzlichen Zeitzeugen, verdanke ich unbürokratische Unterstützung und grundlegende Auskünfte. Immer hilfreich: Antonin Doukopil vom Bauamt. Norbert Schmidt war unverzichtbarer Ratgeber und Übersetzer, Tomáš Valena Mittler zum kulturellen Hintergrund. Auf Ausdauer und Sorgfalt von Verlag und Grafikbüro strobo B M war so Verlass wie auf das Engagement und genaue Auge Petra Steiners, Fotografin.
Wichtigen Vorarbeiten sind zu nennen: An erster Stelle ist Petr Volf mit mehreren Publikationen, voran „A renaissance town of modern architecture“, Litomyšl 2014; dann Milan Skrivánek, Pavel Vopálka, „Litomyšl, eine ehrwürdige Stadt“, Litomyšl 1994. Unentbehrlich waren zahlreiche Gespräche. Ein Hinweis zum Schluss: Die ungewöhnlich sorgfältig bearbeitete Internetseite der Stadt Litomyšl „LAM Litomyšl“ (lam.litomysl.cz) ist als Vertiefung unbedingt zu empfehlen.
Florian Aicher

ACKNOWLEDGEMENTS

It was Matthias Mulitzer, architect, who first told me about Litomyšl. I owe much to the community and its mayors – irreplaceable contemporary witnesses – for their unconditional support. Always helpful: Antonin Doukopil from the Building Department. Norbert Schmidt was an indispensable advisor and translator, Tomas Valena helped me with the cultural background. The persistence and care of the publisher and the graphic studio strobo B M was as reliable as the commitment and close eye of photographer Petra Steiners. Important preliminary work should be mentioned; Petr Volf comes first with several publications, most notably “a renaissance town of modern architecture“, Litomyšl 2014; then Milan Skrivánek, Pavel Vopálka, “Litomyšl, eine ehrwürdige Stadt“, Litomyšl 1994. Many conversations we had were indispensable. A final note: the carefully edited website of the town of Litomyšl, “LAM Litomyšl“ (lam.litomysl.cz), is exceptional and highly recommendable as an additional source.
Florian Aicher

BILDNACHWEIS / PICTURE CREDITS

Fotografen / Photographers **Seite** / Page

Boháč, Matěj: 44, 46, 47
BoysPlayNice: 68, 72, 73
Getzel, Ondřej: 104
Havlová, Ester: 70, 74, 76, 77
Hejzlar, Jaroslav: 106, 109, 110, 111
Horák, Jaroslav: 43, 126
Malý, Jan: 87, 116, 121, 122, 123
Markel, Benedikt: 71
Polák, Petr: 142, 144, 145
Renza, František: 62 unten / bottom, 78, 81
101 unten / bottom
Šlapal, Filip: 64, 66, 139, 140, 141
Souček, Tomáš: 48, 52, 53, 54, 56, 57, 115
Steiner, Petra: 1. Einführungsbild (Vorsatz / endpaper front), 2. Einführungsbild (Vorsatz / endpaper front), 12, 13, 18, 19 oben / top, 24, 25, 26, 27, 30, 31, 36, 37, 42, 62 oben, 84, 86, 88, 89, 94, 96, 97, 98, 99, 100, 101 oben links / top left, 101 oben rechts / top right, 105, 1. Schlussbild (Nachsatz / endpaper back), 2. Schlussbild (Nachsatz / endpaper back)
Tláskalová, Nikola: 19 Mitte / middle, 117
Vojáček, Michele: 67
Vopálka, Pavel: 19 unten / bottom, 51, 58, 60, 61, 80, 82, 83, 102, 112, 114, 118, 127, 128, 130, 131, 132, 135, 136, 138
Židlický, David: 90, 92, 93, 124

Autor / Author
Florian Aicher

Projektleitung / Project management
Sandra Hofmeister

Redaktion / Editorial team
Signe Decker, Lucia Gruber, Michaela Linder, Jasmin Rankl, Maria Remter

Lektorat (Deutsch) / Copy-editing (German)
Katrin Pollems-Braunfels

Übersetzung, Lektorat (Englisch)
Translation, Copy-editing (English)
Stefan Widdes

Gestaltung / Design
strobo B M (Matthias Friederich, Julian von Klier, Monnier Ostermair)

Illustration Cover / Cover illustration
Kai Meyer

Zeichnungen / Drawings
Tina Wagner, Sabrina Heckel

Reproduktion / Reproduction
Repro Ludwig, AT-5700 Zell am See

Druck und Bindung / Printing and binding
druckpruskil.gmbh

Die für dieses Buch verwendeten FSC-zertifizierten Papiere werden aus Fasern hergestellt, die nachweislich aus umwelt- und sozialverträglicher Herkunft stammen.
The FSC-certified paper used for this book is manufactured from fibres -originating from environmentally and -socially compatible sources.

DETAIL Business Information GmbH,
München / Munich
detail.de
detail-online.com

ISBN 978-3-95553-486-8 (Print)
ISBN 978-3-95553-487-5 (E-Book)

Bibliografische Information der Deutschen Nationalbibliothek: Die Deutsche Nationalbibliothek verzeichnet diese Publikation in der Deutschen Nationalbibliografie; detaillierte bibliografische Daten sind im Internet über dnb.d-nb.de abrufbar.

Bibliographical information published by the German National Library. The German National Library lists this publication in the Deutsche Nationalbibliografie; -detailed bibliographical data are available on the internet at dnb.d-nb.de.

MIX
Papier aus verantwortungsvollen Quellen
FSC® C014340
FSC www.fsc.org

Litomyšl
moderní historické město